In the Shadow of Islam

By the same author

The Oblivion Seekers

Isabelle Eberhardt

In the Shadow of
Islam

Translated and with a Preface by
Sharon Bangert

Peter Owen • *London & Chester Springs PA*

PETER OWEN PUBLISHERS
73 Kenway Road London SW5 0RE
Peter Owen books are distributed in the USA by
Dufour Editions Inc. Chester Springs PA 19425–0449

Translated from the French *Dans l'ombre chaude de l'Islam*
First published by Editions Fasquelle, Paris
First published in Great Britain 1993
Translation and Preface © Sharon Bangert 1993

ISBN 0–7206–0889–9

A catalogue record for this book is available from the British Library

Printed and made in Great Britain by
Biddles of Guildford and King's Lynn

Preface

Among the following pages, in the chapter entitled 'Looking Back', the author says, 'For me it seems that by advancing into unknown territories, I enter into my life.' This book recounts Isabelle Eberhardt's ultimate advance. Courage and hunger for an authentic life led her into territories both outside her and within: she was captivated by the Sahara and its inhabitants; but the same sense of adventure led her also on an interior journey, where lay the true goal of her search, and the safe harbour from buffetings by chance.

Isabelle Eberhardt lived her first nineteen years in Geneva, born there in 1877. Her mother was the wife of an aristocratic Russian general named De Moerder, but she eloped to Switzerland with her children's tutor, Alexander Trophimowsky, a former Russian Orthodox priest turned anarchist. Trophimowsky was Isabelle's father, though neither he nor her mother acknowledged the fact. Instead, Isabelle always called him 'Vava', or great-uncle. Trophimowsky gave Isabelle her mother's maiden surname and directed her upbringing, schooling her in the nonconformism which would mark her entire life. He had her wear boy's clothes, learn to ride, work alongside her brothers at toughening, outdoor labour, and willingly taught her Arabic at her request. Trophimowsky imparted to Isabelle, however painfully for her, the moral and physical stamina her later life would demand; for his tactics from the start ensured that Isabelle would be ill suited and ill equipped for life in middle-class European society. In North Africa she would conduct herself nearly everywhere and always as an Arab and a man. Traditional Arab courtesy and discretion led native North Africans to respect her masquerade, though they were never taken in by it. But for Isabelle to pull it off must have required of her a considerable degree of self-assurance and singleness of purpose, particularly as her disguise never prevented her from taking numerous lovers from among the French military and native troops, and even, eventually, an Arab husband.

Although it was unconventional, Isabelle felt her home life to be restrictive and gloomy. She would gaze with fascination at the long road, white in the moonlight, curving away from the Villa Neuve, as their house was called, and dream of elsewhere. As she would later write in her diary, 'As always, I feel a boundless sadness, an inarticulate longing for something I cannot describe, a nostalgia for a *place* for which I have no name.'

Perhaps influenced to some extent by the orientalism gripping Europe at the time, and already attracted to Islam, Isabelle, accompanied by her mother, sailed for Tunis in 1897. There they both officially became Muslims. Her mother died six months later, leaving Isabelle morbidly bereaved until Trophimowsky arrived and responded to her suicidal ravings by offering her his pistol, which she refused.

Isabelle lived on in Tunis, impressing some (by her intelligence), scandalizing others (with her *kif*-smoking and sexual promiscuity), until she had to return to Geneva to replenish her funds. Trophimowsky died around this time, leaving his estate to Isabelle. However, his will was contested by a surviving wife in Russia, and Isabelle was too naïve, too impatient, or both, to remain in Geneva to supervise the legal settlement, and thus forfeited most of her inheritance.

Around the middle of August 1900, at El Oued in the

Algerian desert, Isabelle met the man whom she would marry, Slimène Ehnni. He was a quartermaster in the *spahis*, a regiment of native troops under French command in which Slimène's brothers, father, and uncles had also served. Isabelle's attachment to Slimène was marked from the first by a combination of desperate need and fatalistic pessimism about their prospects together. She clung to him as her only family, her best friend. She also saw him as 'the only true Muslim' of all the men she had known, 'for he loves Islam with all his heart and is not content with paying it mere lip service'. Slimène was a member of the Kadriya, the first and oldest of the Sufi orders, to which Isabelle was also initiated. Their relationship was punctuated by frequent and lengthy separations, due partly to his military orders and partly to Isabelle's wanderlust, as well as to the fact that Isabelle was for a time expelled from the French North African colonies.

The cause of her expulsion was an assassination attempt made on her in January 1901, by a fanatic member of a non-Sufi cult, the Tidjanya. The attack occurred in Behima, near El Oued. She was in the company of her Sufi brethren, in a house belonging to one of them, and engaged in translating a telegram for a local tradesman. The hood of her burnous was covering her turban, her head bent in concentration, so that she could not see the stranger rush up with a sword. His blow was blocked by a laundry line above her head, sparing her skull the full impact, but her left elbow was cut to the bone. A number of speculations have been put forth about the assassin's motive. Isabelle's own testimony to the investigating authorities held that he was in the pay of the Tidjanya sect whose hatred for the Kadriyas was well known: she was a choice target because of her popularity among the Tidjanyas' enemies. Isabelle quickly forgave the assassin, Abdallah, insisting that it was not he who should stand trial, but those who were behind him.

Upon being released from a six-week hospital stay, Isabelle

was ordered by the French to leave Algeria. Her presence was doubtless seen by the authorities as provocative, and her activities dangerous to herself as well as to colonial law and order. Isabelle set off for Marseilles to stay with her brother Augustin and his wife, whose finances were quite as strained as Isabelle's own. She was, to her surprise, commanded to return to Algeria in June for Abdallah's trial. This occasioned her some distress in wondering what to wear. She was sensitive to the fact that it was her Arab men's dress which had to a great extent provoked both Abdallah's attack and the hostility of the French military authorities. She decided first on European men's dress, writing to Slimène, 'I don't care if I dress as a workman, but to wear ill-fitting, cheap and ridiculous women's clothes, no, never. . . .' But when the day came, she appeared in native women's dress, asserting in answer to the defence lawyer's question, that she normally wore male attire because it was more practical for riding.

Abdallah's death sentence was commuted to hard labour for life, and was protested by Isabelle who declared in a letter to the court her pity for Abdallah, his wife, and children. A later appeal by her resulted in a further reduction of his sentence to ten years' imprisonment.

But even before the trial concluded, she was again served with an order of expulsion from Algeria. From May to October she lived with Augustin and his wife in Marseilles and, still dressed as a man, worked as a stevedore as best she could with her disabled arm. Otherwise she spent her time writing her journal, a novel, and numerous letters to Slimène. During this period, the impact of her brush with death stimulated her religious and mystical feelings. She came to view Abdallah as the heavenly emissary he had claimed to be, because of the effect his action had on her inner life.

Finally, in August, Slimène was transferred to Marseilles, and by October he and Isabelle were married in a French civil ceremony. Their union bestowed French citizenship upon

Isabelle (Slimène was already a naturalized French citizen) along with the right to return to Algeria, which they did in January 1902. The following months were spent living at first with Slimène's family in Bône, then in Algiers. Isabelle was sometimes thrilled to be living the life of a 'hermit', alternately pleased to sample again the conversation of intellectuals. In Algiers, she met Victor Barrucand, a journalist: 'A modern mind, subtle and perceptive, but biased by the notions of his time', as Isabelle described him. A couple of months later, she began to see him as 'a dilettante in the domain of thought and even more so when it comes to feeling, a spiritual nihilist in other words'. However, she also recognized him as a practical man 'who knows how to handle himself', a quality Isabelle lacked, by her own admission.

Though so recently reunited with Slimène, Isabelle was soon taking to the road alone, to visit *zawiyas* – Sufi schools or centres of learning – in unexplored regions. She was commissioned by Barrucand to contribute a series of articles for *Les Nouvelles*, which he edited. Barrucand also helped Slimène obtain a position following his military discharge.

Slimène's new post was that of *khodja*, or interpreter-secretary to the administration at Ténès, a town on the Algerian coast, one hundred miles west of Algiers. Here the couple were able to enjoy for the first time a period of relative financial security, and a few good friendships, including that of the writer Robert Randau. However, the colonials in Ténès soon came to rub Isabelle the wrong way. For her they were 'pretentious Philistines who strut about sporting tight trousers and silly hats'. They, for their part, must have found Isabelle's ways a constant irritant. Moreover, Isabelle and Slimène were drawn against their will into local political intrigues, which eventually drove Isabelle back to Algiers to help Barrucand edit his new magazine *El Akhbar*. Slimène, unwilling to carry on alone, resigned his position in April 1903.

This opened a new phase in Isabelle's life which coincided with a new phase in North African political affairs. In 1903 General Hubert Lyautey was posted to Algeria, in charge of pushing France's influence westward into Morocco. Lyautey was an imaginative man, with more original ideas on colonization than his military colleagues in North Africa. He cast France's mission in completely new terms, with a goal of 'pacific penetration' rather than military conquest of Morocco. His liberal views were championed by Barrucand in *El Akhbar*, and he wrote to Lyautey about Isabelle. He promoted her as someone uniquely equipped to advance their cause and possibly gather intelligence among the native Muslims: a French citizen, married to a gallicized Muslim, familiar with native language, religion, and customs, and enormously trusted by Arabs and Berbers alike. Her Kadriya membership gave her access to places where no other European dared venture. Barrucand proposed to Isabelle that she go to the district south of Oran to report on army activities, the insurgent tribes, and to describe the as yet unknown territory. Isabelle enthusiastically agreed, and set off for the southern desert by railway. Slimène, meanwhile, had taken up a new post, this time as *khodja* in Guergour, another northern town.

When Isabelle and Lyautey met in October they quickly became friends. Lyautey shared Isabelle's attraction to Islam, mysticism, and Africa, and admired her rebelliousness, her rejection of 'prejudice, servitude and banality'. Isabelle seemed to respect Lyautey's attitudes and his quick grasp of local issues. In some of her articles from this period, her reports reflect his views. But despite her friendly intimacy with the general, she continued to prefer the company of soldiers – legionnaires and native *mokhazni* – enthusiastically exchanging stories with them in the cafés, whatever their language.

She returned north in December 1903, to spend Ramadan

with Slimène. There seems to have been a break in their relations, though, for she left again abruptly in February 1904 for Ain Sefra: Lyautey's headquarters and her stepping stone to the south and west. Many reminiscences among the following pages date from this period of living native-style, sleeping under the stars or on the floor of a Moorish café, intoxicated by the vastness of the desert. Perhaps only the Sahara could give her the physical distance from Europe's social mores to match the psychological distance she had always lived with.

We know from his letters that Lyautey desired an alliance with Sidi Brahim, the *marabout* of Kenadsa, site of a major centre for Sufi studies in North Africa. Sidi Brahim's influence in the region was so great that France regarded his friendly rapport as a *sine qua non* for 'pacifying' the dissident, war-like tribes. Isabelle's decision to go to Kenadsa and take up residence at its *zawiya* seems likely to have been at Lyautey's urging. Her presence there would have been convenient for his purposes of gathering information and promoting the French cause to the *marabouts*. From Isabelle's point of view, Lyautey's endorsement of her journey would have been equally convenient, and there is no evidence that Isabelle went to Kenadsa for any but her own reasons. 'The Marabout's Indignation', 'Saharan Theocracy', 'Garden Meal', and 'African Influences' contain, to varying degrees, glimpses of the political situation at the time. They show Isabelle sympathetic to local laws and customs and convinced that European conquest of Africa was doomed.

Kenadsa was not the first *zawiya* Isabelle had frequented, but it was doubtless the most important, not only for its spiritual prestige and traditions, but also for the fateful timing of her arrival there, in terms of her own development. Although on one level the following narrative is a travel journal, it is distinctive for what is omitted. For instance, we don't know that she is headed for Kenadsa until she actually arrives there. She would have been obliged by the esoteric tradition to remain silent about the instruction she received at the *zawiya*, and the inner tension established by the secret affects the style of her writing. She turns outwards: towards the surrounding landscape, the comings and goings of Kenadsa's inhabitants and nomadic neighbours, the quotidian events within the *zawiya* which were not forbidden to tell. Yet to these observations she brings a heightened sensitivity to their detail and to their significance; the reader begins to anticipate the *aperçu* at the end of chapters, the resolution uniting object with subject, observer with observed.

The shift in Isabelle's attitude toward Slimène can be noted at many points in these pages. 'To live alone is to live free', she writes from the road in 'Looking Back'; ' . . . I will suffer no more from anyone'. And by the close of her stay at Kenadsa she would write, in 'Reflections on Love', that she had found 'a great talisman', whether imparted to her from her teachers, or composed in her own heart: 'Never give your soul to a creature, because it belongs to God alone; see in all creatures a motive for rejoicing, in homage to the Creator; never seek yourself in another, but discover yourself in yourself.' Solitude, which formerly had been her crucible, was transformed into a gift and a necessity, a state in which she could be at peace.

Isabelle had intended to stay at Kenadsa all summer, and it is clear from what she writes that her departure was premature, though the date is unknown. Her hospitalization in Ain Sefra did not begin until 2 October, and she wrote to Slimène on the 16th asking him to come down for her release. He arrived by the 20th, rejoining his wife after a separation of eight months. She had rented a rude, clay house near the riverbed where she went to meet Slimène after releasing herself from hospital around eight in the morning. By midday the town was ripped apart by a torrent of yellow flood water – completely unexpected, the weather having been mild. All

[12]

the lower part of the town was swept away. Slimène some-how escaped; Isabelle's body was found inside the shut house, wedged behind a fallen beam under the staircase. Lyautey took charge of her burial, and ordered a thorough search of the flood's debris for her manuscripts.

The text of the following pages, which Isabelle referred to as her 'Sud-Oranais' stories, was discovered in an urn and sent by Lyautey to Victor Barrucand. Grieving, Barrucand addressed Isabelle in a note written at a visit to her grave at Ain Sefra, and retitled the work, saying, 'I want to situate our love *in the warm shadow of Islam*. It's the title that I've given to your Saharan adventure.' He assumed the role of Isabelle's literary executor, and edited her work for publication, attracting sharp criticism for claiming co-authorship when *Dans l'ombre chaude de l'Islam* appeared in 1920.

Hence my task has been to translate Barrucand's words along with Isabelle's. If, as the Italians say, 'to translate is to betray', his was the first betrayal, though well meant. I hope my betrayals have been to Barrucand's emendations rather than to Isabelle's intentions.

For their help to me in the writing of this preface I am particularly indebted to Paul Bowles's *The Oblivion Seekers*; Annette Kobak's *Isabelle: The Life of Isabelle Eberhardt*; and Nina de Voogd's *The Passionate Nomad: The Diary of Isabelle Eberhardt*. I am also very grateful for Sacha Palliser's advice on the meanings of Arabic words within the text.

Sharon Bangert

Departure
Ain Sefra, May 1904

Last year I left this place to the gusts of winter. The town was numbed with cold, and great shrill winds scoured it, bending the fragile nakedness of the trees. Today I see it quite differently, become itself again, in the dismal gleam of summer: very Saharan, very sleepy, with its tawny *ksar* at the foot of the golden dune, its holy *koubbas* and its blue-green gardens.

It is so much the little capital of the Oranian desert, solitary in its sandy valley, between the monotonous immensity of the high plateaux and the southern furnace.

Then, it seemed to me morose, without charm, because the magical sun wasn't there to wrap it in a luminous atmosphere, the chief luxury of African towns. But now that I regard it as a temporary home, I begin to love it. What's more, I vow not to leave it again for some tedious return to the banal Tell, and this enables me to see the town with new eyes. When I leave, it will only be to descend further, towards the great South, where the gravelled plain of the *hamada* sleeps under the eternal sun.

Among the white-trunked poplars, following footpaths along the first undulations of the dune, smelling again the scent of sap and resin, I feel myself lost in a forest. This scent, so sweet and pure, combines sensuously with the distant aroma of flowering acacias. How I love the exuberant greenness, and the trunks, wrinkled as an elephant's skin, and these fig trees swollen with bitter milk, surrounded by buzzing swarms of golden flies! In this garden, so unexpected among all the aridity, I have passed long hours on my back, drunk on warm breezes and the hypnotic oscillation of branches – like a ship's riggings – against the sky.

Beyond the last of the poplars, now grown spindly and stunted, the track of sand climbs, ending abruptly at the foot of the immaculate dune, which seems to be of fine golden powder. There the wind plays freely, building up the hills, hollowing the valleys, opening precipices, creating ephemeral landscapes according to its whim.

At the summit, only slightly more stable with arrises of black stone, a reddish 'blockhaus' watches over the valley; a sentinel with empty eyes that, having witnessed the passage of armies and robbers, looks out now on silence and the peace of vague horizons.

The scorching dune rises stark against the unrelenting blue of Mount Mektar. The day ends gently over Ain Sefra, drowned in soft vapours and fragrant scents. I experience a delicious melancholy, yet am strangely revitalized by my impending departure. All the cares, the heavy malaise of the last months spent in irksome and nerve-wracking Algiers, all that sorrow, my 'blues', is left behind.

In the city, I was forced to scorn things and people when I would have liked to understand everything, excuse everything. To have to defend yourself against stupidity when you have nothing to argue about, nothing to do with it! I don't know anymore ... I'm not interested. ... The sun is still mine, and the beckoning road. This could be, for a while, an entire philosophy.

Once in my life, in a soul that I thought was free, I watched a pure, strong passion grow, and I said to my friend: 'Be careful, when we're happy we cease to understand another's suffering . . .' He set off for happiness, or so he believed, and I toward my destiny. Now I have drawn apart, and I feel my soul regain its health, innocently open to all joys, to all the delicate sensualities of the eyes and of dreams.

I rediscover in the village's only Arab street calm impressions of 'home', which date from the month of Ramadan last year. Many familiar folks, on benches and on mats in front of the coffeehouses. Many friendly greetings to exchange.

And all the time the secret joy of knowing that I will leave tomorrow at dawn, leave all these things which are still pleasing and dear to me this evening. Who except a nomad, a vagabond, could understand this double rejoicing?

Once more astounded by all that has captured me and all I have left, I tell myself that love is a worry and that what's necessary is to love *to leave* – persons and things being loveliest when left behind.

Before the iron bars and pots of basil in the window of a Moorish café, a crowd begins to form. Pipes are playing there so I go in; this droning, sad music puts an end to my reverie and, more importantly, will excuse me from talking. . . .

Musicians of the West

A square room painted pale blue, with pink panels. To the right, in back, the vaulted oven's smoky plaster, and on wooden shelves, the cups, glasses and plates. A few wooden benches and common tables of rusty iron crowd the café. A captive bird sleeps in its cage.

Strange little Saharan café, frequented by Moroccans and nomads. The audience is packed in. Among the Arabs, in burnous and dirty *haiks*, a few *spahis* and *mokhazni*, native horsemen. Fists on their knees, all wait silently, watching the back of the room where the musicians take their seats on a bench.

These are the Beni Guil of Chott Tigri. With their tatters dyed red, and their sandals, they hardly resemble the singers and musicians of the Algerian high plateaux, who wear pretentious, 'proper' clothes and, affecting an Arab flair, sport embroidered vests and silk turban cords. These musicians of the West are perfect specimens of their rough race, a collar of black ugly beard giving their faces an almost Hindu air.

However, on one of them the coarse veil hanging from his white, flared turban frames a handsome, regular face with an aquiline nose, sensitive nostrils, sad eyes. The other, a flute player, is blind. He puts all his soul into the shrieks and whistles of his pipe. As if he were speaking to it, he rolls the dull globes of his dead eyes, and his torso sways in rhythm to the beat. There's also an old drummer in the troupe, and near him a strange singer, his eyes closed, head sagging as if drunk.

The only luxury these paupers have consists of two flutes. They are ringed with leather and polished copper; blue silk strands and fine silver chains hung with Moroccan coins decorate them.

Symphony of the forbidding *hamada*!

The tambourine's ceaseless, muffled syncope is a human heartbeat now moved, now angered, weakening, tiring, and voluptuously dying. Embellishing this arterial pulse, the harsh flutes ring at times with war marches in which long, mysterious notes are held, seeming to soar, then hum with the murmur of tranquil water or a soothing breeze.

The Beni Guil from around the village invade the room – gauche intruders, desert people amazed by benches and tables. But they smile; they are proud of their brothers' success among the northern renegades. Money clanks into a platter placed on the floor. At each offering, the tambourine

[18]

player rewards the generosity of the giver with a crescendo.

But the Beni Guil are content to encourage the musicians by their attention and exclamations of approval. The rare one resigns himself to throwing a sou on the platter after rummaging a while in his *zaboula*, a kind of moneybag of red leather the nomads carry. But there now – one of them, quite young, rises suddenly and sketches a rhythmic dance, slowly, the end of his knotty stick leaning against his chest. They laugh at his rustic shepherd's movements.

The café owner, his loins girt with a red and green *fouta*, makes the rounds, presenting his steaming beverages on a tray, and each time, at the top of his voice, he names the one who has ordered the tea, calling down on him the blessing of Allah.

Death of a Muslim

The first light of morning spreads on the horizon like a great purple flower. The sand dune, studded with tufts of alfa, glows around the little *koubba* of Sidi Bou Djemaa, which overlooks the road to Beni Yaho and Sfissifa. Pink touches the tops of black fig trees, and large willows weep glistening silver.

All around the *koubba*, Arabs awaken, pilgrims who've come a long way to ask protection of the great saint. They line up, all facing the dawn, praying their long prayers. The beautiful, grave gestures of the Muslim rite exalt even the humblest of them.

Behind the little enclosing wall, women are already chatting around a fire of dead wood – nomads accompanying the men of their tribe. They hardly bother to veil their faces.

Under a tree a madman in rags, leaning on a stick, chants the Koran, getting the verses out of order. He is handsome

[19]

with his emaciated face, his black hair pressed to his forehead by a shred of white linen. His large eyes, ardent and troubled, are transfixed on a point in space.

From time to time the group of women whoop and yell as for a feast day.

But then at the crest of the dune a cortège appears. A few Arabs advance slowly, to the accompaniment of a grave and rhythmic song. Behind this group, four men carry on their shoulders a stretcher draped in white, and at the apparition of this unknown believer setting off toward eternity in the glory of morning, all the shouting ceases.

The men enter the unwalled cemetery. Among the tombs scattered across the sand, among the nameless, dateless gravestones, a hole is dug rapidly, so rapidly in the light sand! And on the edge of this little pit they place the dead man, his face to the sun.

Now, in a semicircle, the Muslims pray their last prayer in a low voice, without prostrations. Quickly, with a simple row of bricks, they bank the grave and plant three green palms in the mounded sand already dispersing in the fresh breeze. Everyone leaves.

How simple it is to die!

Beside me, Si Abdelali, an educated man from Marrakesh, starts softly singing an old dirge of the kind that is all but forgotten.

> Here I am, dead, soul and body divided.
> They have wept over me the ceremonial tears.
> Four men have carried me on their shoulders,
> Attesting their faith in the one God.
> They have carried me to the cemetery,
> They have prayed over me, without prostrating,
> The last of the prayers of this world.
> They've thrown earth on top of me.
> My friends walk away as if they've never known me.

And I rest alone in the darkness of the tomb,
Where there's no joy nor sorrow, no sun nor moon,
My only companion the blind worm.
The tears have dried on my loved ones' cheeks,
And the dry thorns have grown on my grave.
My son has said, 'God have mercy on him!'
He who is gone toward the mercy of God
Is likewise gone from the fellowship of men.
There's no rescue, no reprieve in the land of the dead.
O you who stand before my tomb, don't shake your
    head at my fate.
Once I was just like you;
Someday you'll be just like me.

The air of this complaint is melancholy and sweet, the *taleb*'s voice resonant. I gaze at the small mound abandoned there forever, in the emptiness of the sandy desert.

We headed for Sfissifa, a little Muslim town without a single European, without even a Jew. Again the dark rocks typical of this region and, inside the *ksar*, a shabby life, crumbling clay walls, veiled faces of mummies. Everything fallen to ruins. But we enjoy sound sleep under a spreading pomegranate tree, in the dazzling late-morning sun.

It was there my curiosity recognized you, sickly villagers – pale, whinging, and effeminately dressed – a race weakened by ancient inbreeding and sedentary lives. I saw you again, villages crumbling in the shade of delightful gardens, invaded by desert little by little, being devoured. And I realized then, there are people, too, who exude decay.

Returning from Sfissifa we see the sun disappear, but its great red light still bathes the valley. We pass again before Sidi Bou

Djemaa. A profound silence, a silence one feels, almost an anguish, weighs down the *koubba* and the cemetery. There, among the little anonymous stones are raised a few *marabouts'* tombs, rectangles encrusted with dry earth.

The door to the *koubba* is closed, and before it is seated an old beggar, his stick leaning against the wall. Softly, from the shadow of his blindness, he murmurs words without accent, reciting to himself.

On the height, two *mokhazni* in black burnous have dismounted from their horses and pray, all alone, in the last light of day.

A chained dog offers to the sky his wolf's muzzle and narrow, red eyes, and howls his lamentation, as if from an infinite sadness.

On the Road

After a short, moonlit night spent on a mat in front of the Moorish café in Beni Ounif, I awoke happy, with the euphoria that takes me when I have slept outdoors under the great sky, and when I'm about to set off on a journey.

Seated on a stone at the side of the road, I wait for Djilali ould Bahti, the *mokhazni* who will accompany me on the road to Bechar.

To go to Bechar! Finally to cross the fateful boundary marked by Beni Ounif is enough to make me feel calm and joyful, free of the worry I suffered at Ain Sefra.

Time passes, and this Djilali is late in coming.

The day lengthens, a splendid summer day, without clouds or mist. A fresh breeze since yesterday evening has chased away all dust and haze. The sky opens, infinite, profound, with the green transparency of a tranquil ocean.

At the horizon, in all this golden green, a yellower, brighter gleam increases, soon becoming orange, then red. Ahead, in the dark west, the moon descends, livid. Like the face of a dying man.

Nearby, the great white *koubba* of Sidi Slimane is outlined in gold, on the tarnished-copper colour of the sky. Orange rays bathe the dark earth, the tombs, and the cracked houses.

Finally Djilali arrives and we leave, turning our horses towards the fading moon.

This *mokhazni* is a big brown boy, one of the good, honest Trafi tribe of nomads from Geryville. He is friendly and quick-witted, and will make a good companion for the road.

We make our way through the valley of black rock, between the Grouz highlands, still shining, and the low burning hills of Gara. On the right we pass the lovely little palm grove of Melias, drowsing at the entrance of a deep gorge in the Grouz mountains. Last year, bands of outlaws made this their watering-stop, these desert gardens so peaceable and welcoming today.

The farther behind we leave sterile Beni Ounif, the more grass appears on the sandy soil. Wadis deepen, full of increasingly verdant bushes. Some large mastic trees — so providential in the scorching wilderness — cast their shadows on the red soil, marking the course of empty hours.

A dust cloud comes on us from the west, with the wind. It is a legionnaire company of blond, deeply tanned men covered with dust, returning from the South singing German *lieder* or Italian *canzone*.

The sick are bedded on the baggage carts. Perched very high, they regard the monotonous landscape with the indifference born of fever, silently calculating the probable hour of arrival at Beni Ounif from where, tomorrow, they'll be transported by train to the hospital at Ain Sefra.

An hour passes. We join up with a small convoy of wagons escorted by riflemen. The men have removed their bags and their rifles and loaded them on to the carts; they march non-chalantly, with the small steps of mules, as if out for a stroll.

They pass. We fall back into the silence of the road.

From time to time Djilali begins a song, which he never finishes.

There's little wind; we turn our backs to the sun. The heat is not overwhelming. We are well, without need of talk.

So it is on the desert roads of the south; long hours without sadness, without worry; vague and restful, where one may live in silence. I have never regretted a single one of these 'lost' hours.

The Drama of Hours

To travel is not to think, but to see things in succession, with one's life sensed in the measure of space. The monotony of landscapes slowly unrolling soothes our cares, infuses us with lightness and quiet, which the fevered traveller could never know on his full-speed excursions. At the unhurried pace of horses stunned by the heat, the smallest accidents of the journey preserve their startling beauty. These are not fretful predicaments; rather, a calm and vital state of mind rules, which once belonged to all human races and is still preserved among us in the blood of nomads.

In Algiers, seeing all the Europeans flocking at the same times to the same side of the arcades, to feel as if they belong, or promenading around the music-filled square, I sense the herd mentality. But not here. I feel it's better to herd sheep than to be part of a crowd, and there's neither arrogance nor romanticism in that statement.

I live this life of the desert as simply as the camel-drivers and the *mokhazni*. I have always preferred simplicity, finding in it vibrant pleasures which I don't hope to explain.

When I sleep under the starry skies of this region, religious in their vastness, I feel penetrated by the earth's energies; a sort of brutality makes me straddle my mare and push straight ahead unthinkingly. I don't want to imagine anything; the stages of the journey only count as insignificant details. In this country without green, in this country of rock, something exists: time. And the spectacle of morning and evening skies.

The Bedouin in his dusty *haik* understands this and says nothing, but he sings. Djilali has never explained to me why he never finishes his songs.

Halt in the Desert

Last year to get to Bechar you'd go towards the east, behind the mountains, to the little outpost of Bou Yala. But it's now abandoned since the military's frontier has pushed west. Now Bou Ayech is the first stop after Beni Ounif, 35 kilometres beyond.

It is ten o'clock and the valley is kindled. Red vapours tremble at the shifting horizon. The heat intensifies. A thin trickle of blood runs from the dried nostrils of our mares. Invaded by languor, I let myself be lulled in my Arab saddle, comfortable as an armchair. Ben Zireg is only 28 kilometres away, and we will have plenty of time to go to bed there, so why should we hurry?

Only by arriving at the 'village' of Bou Ayech can one actually see it, it blends so well with the colour of the soil. About ten frame barracks, a redoubt of yellowish earth, and ten or so shapeless Arab huts made of brushwood, where the Moroccan railway workers lodge. One hundred metres away all this blends with the alfa and the dust, and this corner of the valley seems as deserted as any other.

The line of the state railway stops these days a few kilometres beyond Bou Ayech, giving an air of commercial vitality to this forlorn outpost.

Already here the countryside is looking both more Saharan and less dismal than at Beni Ounif; the pale sand, under the gilt-green mantle of alfa, contrasts sharply with the tortured, black *hamada* of Ounif.

In one of the village barracks, some Spaniards drink anisette at a wooden table. With roughly hewn faces, shaved, tanned and hardened, with big hats of black felt, boleros and espadrilles – they are a rough, rude race, inured to solitude and privation under the harshest of suns.

From a window in the wall of the barrack a pay-clerk distributes wages to the workers. I notice that these have almost all abandoned their handsome native clothing for the dreadful European cast-offs of the *trabadjar*, which clash with their large white turbans.

Here are some exotic northern Moroccans, with their bearded and energetic faces: regular, strong features, and long, fierce eyes. I notice among these workers a few blond, blue-eyed Berbers, of the type one meets in Kabylie, obviously resulting from a distant infusion of Vandal blood.

Only the Figuigians and the people of Tafilala keep to their Arab clothes. As temporary workers, they simply earn a few sous then return straight away to their district.

Bou Ayech provided a rest for us. We were cooking potatoes in the sand, not far from the military huts and the Moorish cafe, in the circular shade of beautiful mastic trees as big as oaks. Soon some men dressed in jerseys and grey berets circled round us, under the eye of the legionnaires. I recognized among them some rejects from the army, of the lowest degree; military outcasts, they are employed in public works at the furthest outposts. Some were naked to the waist, adding to the savagery of this savage world with their extraordinary Parisian tattoos inscribed with grim, revolting, or obscene devices.

Out of boredom, the rejects and the legionnaires come to talk to us. I'm entertained at first, and it's hard not to laugh hearing them say among themselves: 'He's good looking, the little *spahi*; he has fine skin!'

A few *mokhazni* join us. They are from Beni Ounif and I recognize some friendly faces from last year. We invite them for coffee prepared in a mess-tin, and we chat like southerners, in short answers, with simple, inoffensive jokes.

Some Doui Menia camel drivers camped on the heights come to sit beside us. The *mokhazni* tease them, ridiculing their bizarre speech. The nomads answer as best they can, without apparent anger. But underneath, one clearly senses the old hatred dividing the people of the Algerian plateaux from the Moroccans.

The camel drivers finally leave, and the *mokhazni* start preparing their *mella* – the bread of Saharan travellers. One of them mixes flour with water from the goatskin and kneads the mixture on a folded knapsack. Djilali digs a hole in the sand with his hands while the others carry armfuls of wood.

'Mella', declares a Trafi cavalier, 'is to men what alfa is to horses: it keeps you lean, but tough.'

In the evening, the petty officers of the First Foreign who saw me last year on an excursion to Hadjerath M'guil, recognized me and invited me to join them at dinner. The occasion was memorable, not least because though they know quite well who I am, they still scrupulously respected my masculine disguise.

We lingered for trivial conversation, for the sole pleasure of talking of the Saharan country, of the *bled*, of troop

[27]

movements, of construction works, of the future of this lost corner of Earth.

That evening, after their field mess, I was feeling like the soul mate of a southern soldier. I took an unabashed interest in these brave men's stories, as enjoyable as fireside tales at a farmhouse after a long day's hike through the countryside.

Owing to times like these, I carry families, hearths, and campfires in my memory. In hours of isolation and day-dream, they all come back for the duration of a smoke, and these memories are a more bracing tonic for me than those of former enthusiasms (followed by depressions), or than hopes invested in persons that finish always, almost always, in disillusionment and bankruptcy.

This has led me to the conclusion that we should never seek happiness. Along the way it sometimes visits, but always through an inversion. At times I have even recognized it.

Now the night sleeps all blue on the calm of the valley. At the redoubt the Legion's bugle plays its slow, sad command to extinguish the fires.

In these little isolated outposts, when one is silent and alone, the ringing in of evening has something poignant about it; afterwards, you feel the desert all around you.

The last sounds and the last lights are extinguished. I fall asleep in an infinite well-being. Tomorrow I'll set off for different country, and who knows if I will ever return to sleep here, at the foot of this redoubt, in the midst of this landscape.

Ben Zireg

We leave Bou Ayech in the freshness before dawn. The waning moon swims in a greenish sky, and its feeble, sad light glides over the black stones of the trail. Djilali (the dreamer) ends up telling me that it would be better to wait for day before attempting the gorges of Ben Zireg, the old nomads' passage.

We dismount in a wide riverbed which is shallow and dry. Leaving the horses to graze in the alfa, we lie down on the fine sand for a light nap.

We awaken in full daylight, and find we've slept in a charming site. Wild bushes, their flowers forming delicate violet clusters, rise out of the green swell of alfa, and there are wide silvery patches of lavender and wormwood. In the shade of tall mastic trees, asters scatter their little mauve stars: it's such a prodigality of flowers, of vegetal life in the midst of *hamada*.

We enter the tortuous, hollowed-out gorges where the road overhangs a deep wadi. Travelling between high red cliffs, we soon emerge in the valley of Ben Zireg.

What an unforgettable, desolate sight at our exit from the gorges! The grimmest, most doleful of all the desert scenes of the south extends before us.

Between the sharp spur of Djebel Bechar and the high wall of the Antar, a saw-tooth mountain chain encloses the valley which slopes gently toward the wadi. And everything – the hills, the soil of crushed slate, the rugged stones – is black, an olive-black, murky as rotten liver. At the foot of the hills that dominate Bechar, the redoubt, ghastly white, accentuates the horror of this dark landscape.

The 'village' contains no more than a few hovels, military canteens and Moorish cafés.

On the opposite bank of the wadi are aligned the wooden crosses of the Christian cemetery. Not a shadow, not a blade of grass, only two or three meagre date palms in the riverbed.

A kind of hell, from which a poet's imagination could summon the hosts of the dead. Nothing will ever grow in this cursed place. What misanthrope, what superhuman lover of sterile solitude, what sublime madman or monster would consent to live here, facing these sooty hills, in this scorched, bleak circle?

Conflicting impressions of grandeur and foreboding: Ben Zireg resembles those fatal countries seen in bad dreams. Somewhere in *The Thousand and One Nights* there is a landscape like this, of basalt, inhabited by a black giant in chains. The most outrageous flight of an opium hallucination could never achieve this funereal mineral splendour.

The heat becomes overwhelming. Flies swarm round our eyes. I gag at the blast from this oven, and clutch Souf's reins fearfully as we enter this ultimate barrenness.

We await evening anxiously. The day ends steamily, like a conflagration, the redoubt blazing like a glowing ingot. And during the brief instants of nightfall, this dark corner of Ben Zireg seems beautiful, with the staggering beauty of apotheosis.

Then, suddenly, it is finished. Abruptly, night falls, full, misty, rich in mystery, and velvety as warm wings.

We bed down before a Moorish café, on a mat. I will leave before day, to preserve of Ben Zireg my last vision of it at evening.

Water of Lies

Today the going will be long. We will have to walk hours, slowly, at the patient, regular pace of our mares.

Since we left the circle of Ben Zireg, the valley, otherwise unchanging, has widened; here and there a wadi with a little greenery and lovely mastic trees; then, once again, dust and rocks to infinity.

At Hassi en Nous, the half-way point, we stop for lunch and afterwards go to take coffee with the *mokhazni* from the

Bel Haouari post. They are *Rzain* nomads of the Saida circle, and are camped under some makeshift huts. They are easily recognized to be soldiers, these gallant men who, in the desert, have again put on their dusty bedouin burnous.

Beyond Bel Haouari, we travel towards the immense and glowing horizon between a double chain of hills whose odd shapes are amusing. As a traveller is expected to be inquisitive, I ask my companion the name of this geological formation.

'Look closely', he says, 'and you will see why people around here call it Bezaz el Kelba': the dog's teats.

A little farther on he pointed out a black line in the flat valley: the palm grove of Ouagda.

Under the blazing sun, perspective becomes deformed. Impossible to gauge distances: a kind of dizziness blurs our vision while still, to the right and left, the fantastic Bezaz el Kelba. The least variations in the terrain affect the light and cause my eyes either pain or relief.

After the region of stones a zone of pure sand opens up. For the first time south of Oran I'm revisited by the profound impression I first had of other Saharan regions. I recognize it in all its splendour, with its gloomy enchantments and fairies; the earth swooning under the long solar caress; the absence of any geologic shocks; none of the immense effort of mountains.

Suddenly the horizon flickers, the distances are rearranged, and the rusty sand disappears. A great swathe of blue water spreads afar, with date palms reflected in it.

The water reflects the sun, infinitely pure. Djilali begins to laugh, like the big child he is.

'Si Mahmoud, see how the *srab* [mirage] mocks our thirst! If we hadn't anything but this cursed water of lies to wet our lips, we might really be in trouble . . . or have to suck the dog's teats!'

At the edge of the chimeric lake, a troupe of red horsemen advances. Above their closed ranks, a great scarlet standard flutters in the wind. Then they disappear. These were actually donkeys returning to Ouagda, and what we took for the flag was a Saharan well from which the mirage had picked up some shreds of purple.

We travel the length of the Ouagda palm grove, between the small tombs scattered along the way. Ahead, a rust-coloured dune with a white smear at its base: the fortress of Collomb. Bechar, Taagda, Collomb, all these different names can be confusing. In fact, Bechar is the name of the region, as it is of the mountain which blocks the horizon. Taagda is the *ksar* and the larger palm grove above Ouagda. 'Collomb', a foreign name, designates the village under construction.

Our arrival at Bechar revives in me nostalgic memories of Oued Rir and the salt lagoons south of Constantine, another land of fever and mirage.

Oasis Perfume

The mysterious lake has disappeared. In the distance only a few pools remain, azure tatters strewn about in the tawny sand. But now the shade of the palm grove attracts our horses. We finally come to the crowded vaults of the date palms, and the horses stretch their bleeding noses toward the real water, entering the wide river up to their knees among the rushes.

What relief, what totally physical joy – to reach shade, where the breeze is fresh, where our suffering eyes can rest on the deep green of the lush palms, on the pomegranates' blood-red flowers and on the clumps of laurel roses.

After the water of lies, a taste of truth.

We stretch out on the ground, not wanting to enter the *ksar* until evening, after a siesta.

Djilali falls asleep, and I look at this new scenery resembling others I've loved, which have revealed to me the mysterious charm of the oasis. I also recognize here the faint odour of saltpetre, so peculiar to the humid palm groves, this odour of cut fruit which spices all the other scents of life in the shade.

In the deep quiet of this isolated clearing, innumerable emerald lizards and changeable chameleons bathe in patches of sun on the rocks.

No bird-song, no insect cries. What wonderful silence! Everything sleeps in a heavy trance, and the sparse rays glide between the high trunks of the date palms like seduction in a dream.

Looking Back

To live alone is to live free. I no longer want to care about anything. Over the course of months I will place my soul apart. I have known so many days when I lived like a stray dog. Those days are far off, behind vast solitudes, behind crushing mountains, beyond the arid high plateaux and the cultivated Tell, anguished nights in town where worries tumbled behind my eyes, where my heart ached with pity and impotence. Now I have won back my pride, and friendly faces are kinder to me. I will suffer no more from anyone.

Little rue du Soudan where I laboured with head bent over papers, in my faience-tiled room, on a high terrace where linens dried in the sun, with unknown lodgers for neighbours. I'll no longer listen for noises on the stairs; I expect no friend, and my hours are no more than moments of light!

The words I used to write on the margins of letters were bitter ones; but I have left all the letters and the mementoes behind me. Likewise, I've no idea when the papers come out, or of the latest news. The tabloids will reach me from the bureau at Collomb. I will know, but only from time to time, what happens elsewhere; thus I will have more leisure to live by myself. For me it seems that by advancing into unknown territories, I enter into my life.

This road was long and dreary, but we went on: it was enough.

Bechar

At Bechar, at the foot of the dune, the valley slopes almost unnoticeably toward the green belt of the wadi. On the bank, behind the big cemeteries where the wind and camels' footsteps gradually erase the graves, is the old *ksar* of Taagda. Flanked by square towers, surrounded by high, grey walls, solid except for low vaulted doors, Taagda has the sullen air of a citadel.

Inside we follow decrepit lanes; long, covered passages so dark that at the height of noon we have to walk gropingly. Where are the beautiful lines and the full curves of Figuig? Here, it's a jumble. The tall brick houses press against one another and against the streets.

In Bechar, as in all the settlements, everything sleeps, everything collapses. Its exhausted activity fades slowly, the sources of energy are used up, and a heavy, agonized somnolence dampens all attempts at living, whether sedentary or labouring, here in the midst of deserts belonging rightfully to nomads.

The people of Bechar (black Kharatines for the most part, but Arab-speaking) are silent and mistrustful. Even they have a little of the Moroccan arrogance, of revulsion for people from the east, the *M'zanat*; however, they are villagers: pitiable truck gardeners, and not men of the sand.

Last year, because of their isolation, Taagda and Ouagda

were raided by skirmishers. This year, reassured a little, the villagers' courage returns, and they return to their gardens.

The centre of the new 'town' of Collomb is still nothing but a chaos of unfinished battlements, of materials and plaster debris. More ugly slums of mud, whitened to the colour of the pale earth. In all the posts below Oran, such hovels are built in haste to shelter canteens, shops, and Moorish cafés.

Spanish and Jewish elements dominate, here as elsewhere, in the new country. The Jews of Kenadsa, dressed in shabby outfits of green or black, come to set up their ragged tents, and waste no time lighting their little forges for transforming the officers' and *spahis*' money into jewellery.

The gardens of Bechar bring me back to an earlier time, in the wadi of unforgettable Bou Saada, the pearl of the South. There, squatting on the pebbled bank, women veiled in blue or black *mlahfa* washed tattered clothing, beating it with palm stalks. . . . Yes, it's definitely the Bou Saada wadi in the luminous days of summer which these sleepy palm groves of Bechar evoke, but with a note more distant, more sombre – the Moroccan note.

In these gardens, under blossoming pomegranates and the sickly shade of fig trees, delightful corners may be found where the sea-green vaults of the date palms glow with the mystery of true forests. Irrigation *seguias* gurgle in the close-cropped grass, and on all sides the sad little voice of the southern toad pipes its unique note, repeated on and on, out to the arid dunes on the Kenadsa road, out to the last *seguia*, half-choked with sand.

*   *   *

The Black Stallion

This evening, a sky of sanguine clouds over the emptiness of the plain. Beyond the wadi, on the edge of the desert, a heap of wall-slabs, foundations of battered towers: it's the ancient *ksar* of Zekkour, destroyed by the Black Sultan. The enduring debris slowly manages to crumble under the sun and serves as a hideout for tribes of poisonous scorpions and vipers.

We pass slowly before this desolation, and then another, startling, sight comes into view. On the edge of the road, a black mass is struggling, suffering. As we pass, this carcass gathers itself for a jerky effort: a horse, its two rear legs broken, agonizing there, all alone, in the dying evening.

The black stallion raises itself on two uncertain legs thrown out in front; his chest heaves, and he stretches out his bleeding nostrils towards our mares.

Suddenly his large eyes, formerly glazed, light up and he forces a long whinny, a last tender cry toward the shivering females, a cry of revolt and of pain.

Djilali takes out his rifle and aims at the dying beast. One brutal, dry crack from the gun. The black stallion rolls on the red earth, his troubled gaze, his last cry of passion shattered. And unthinkingly Djilali says, with his hearty, childish laugh, 'He is lucky, that one, he died a lover.'

Night falls on the devastation of Zekkour, and on the corpse of the black stallion.

Legionnaires and Mokhazni

On the height, the redoubt of Bechar with its low clay walls, its wide doors under guard, and inside: building materials, piles of stones, all the chaos of a market-town under construction.

We enter the spacious courtyard where the thin little horses belonging to the government are fettered, lazily munching on stale hay. Under shelter of their huts, the *mokhazni* crouch or lie on the ground, their heads resting on their saddles, rifles near to hand, cartridge pouches folded on their soiled tunics. They laugh, they joke, they sing, awaiting casually the order to leave and – who knows? – perhaps never to return.

What does it matter! They are confident, they take refuge in their destiny, they believe that what is written must come to pass whatever they do, and they live their lives. Fatalism is not always a weakness. The only time they think about death is when they're composing ballads.

The Arab understands manly honour, and he wants to die bravely, facing the enemy; but he is absolutely innocent of the desire for posthumous glory. These fellows above all, these rough nomads, know nothing of the search for fame. They voluntarily bring to the service of France their valour, their audacity, and their tireless endurance; they 'serve' loyally, and this is enough for them.

Along with the *mokhazni* there are others, just as insouciant, other lost children, but more complicated – the legionnaires presently engaged in constructing at Bechar the offices for the *Bureau arabe*.

Everywhere, in all the outposts of the southern desert, it's the legionnaires who have raised the first walls; who have energetically and patiently sown the first seeds in the small gardens appearing like magic from the sand. They have built – during troubled days when they had to defend themselves against pillagers, after nights spent listening, under the stress of probable attack.

There's not one wall, not one trench, in Bechar or elsewhere in the country, that was not the work of the Legion. Anonymous work, perhaps harder and more meritorious than the great acts of courage accomplished every day in this profound, echoless country.

There is something, I feel, in the elevation of glory which diminishes courage and which denies some of its beauty. True courage is also ingenuous and tenacious. Its reward is in the joy of action. It's in this sense that these workers have courage, true courage – doubled by a spirit of sacrifice which, unknowingly, saves the world.

Reflections in a Courtyard

Among these brave people I am completely at ease. I entered into their midst and sat down in a corner of the courtyard. They didn't even notice me. Of course, there's nothing remarkable about me. I'm able to pass everywhere completely unobserved, an excellent position to be in for observing. If women are not good at this, it's because their costume attracts attention. Women have always been made to be looked at, and they aren't yet much bothered by the fact. This attitude, I think, gives far too much advantage to men.

I've often been criticized for liking too well the ordinary run of people. But where, I ask, is life, if not among the people? Everywhere else society seems too confined. I sense, in certain circles, an artificial atmosphere; I have trouble breathing. I never know what will be 'correct'. I'm not much troubled, really, by poverty or naïvety, nor even by coarseness. What's really unbearable is the eternal mediocre shame of some people; and the lack of bravery which marks them; their prudence; their pretension to live in a reasonable and well-planned way. In fact, I've always found that this sort ends up in a complete muddle. I've always been astonished to see that a fashionable hat, the right bustline, a pair of stiff

[38]

boots, a little suite of cumbersome little furniture, some silverware and porcelain is enough to quench, in so many people, the thirst for well-being. While very young I was seized by the world's existence and I wanted to know it to its limits. I wasn't made to whirl through intrigues wearing satin blinders. I didn't construct for myself an ideal: I went for discovery. I'm quite aware that this way of life is dangerous, but the moment of danger is also the moment of hope. Besides, I have been penetrated by this idea: that one can never fall lower than oneself. When my heart has suffered, then it has begun to live. Many times on the paths of my errant life, I asked myself where I was going, and I've come to understand, among ordinary folk and with the nomads, that I was climbing back to the sources of life; that I was accomplishing a voyage into the depths of my humanity. In contrast to so many subtle psychologists, I've discovered no new motivations, but I have recapitulated some primal sensations; through all the shabbiness of my adventures, the defining curve of my existence has been expanded.

These words, heartfelt if incoherent, must suffice to explain how I can be interested in such humble things.

Now my eyes are resting on this small courtyard in the Bechar redoubt; they photograph its various aspects; they possess it in its simplicity.

Killing Time

Under a little, tattered tent invaded by flies, someone from Kenadsa has installed a Moorish café. A few government-issue saddles and rifles, and some poor soldiers' clothes lie about, on deposit.

Mokhazni and *spahis* come to this precarious shelter to

drink lukewarm tea and to play interminable games of Spanish *ronda* or dominoes, with the passion all Arabs bring to gaming.

When they play, the sirocco may tear at the tent, the sand may lash their faces, the flies may blind their eyes; nothing, except a call to service, can wrench the players' gazes from their grimy cards or little rectangles of ebony and bone. Cries, laughter – often terrible disputes which, except for their fear of the officers, would end in bloodshed – accompany these games where they spend the greater part of their pay.

We wait for evening, as heedlessly as they.

In this courtyard of the *Bureau arabe* in Bechar, as at Beni Ounif, as everywhere in the south – in the warm shade after prayers, songs rise up, awakening echoes from the dead plain.

The dreaming soul of nomads, reckless and sensual, climbs in wonderful savage songs, raucous at times as cats in the night, and sometimes mild as the gentlest lullaby. Their songs are waves of passion and feeling that cast themselves up on the beach of the sky. Their melancholy breaks on my heart, as well.

Kenadsa

Kaddour ou Barka, chief of the Ziania at Bechar, gave me a negro slave for a guide, named Embarek. We leave the *marabout*'s compound at the pink and green hour of dawn. The weather is clear, with no sign of sirocco. Only a light breeze swells the palm groves at the bottom of the wadi.

The valley we travel, I on horseback and Embarek on foot, stretches between two chains of hills. On the left above us rises the majestic silhouette of the Djebel Bechar.

More blond sand, soft undulations, just the same since the Bezaz el Kelba; the same landscape, the same monotony of

[40]

immense curving lines: no angles, no shocks, no harsh-
ness . . . or almost none.

The farther west we travel, the lower the hills. Alongside
us, on the right, the strange dune crowned with overhanging
rocks, overlooking Bechar. We're a long time passing it while
the sun, now intense, climbs behind us and casts our shadows
on the whitening earth.

Finally we arrive at the summit of a rocky ledge sown with
flint and fragments of slate, like the gloomy valley of Ben
Zireg.

At the horizon, enveloped in pink haze, Kenadsa appears:
some scattered dark splotches of trees, a bluish line which is a
large palm grove, and rising over the sands a squared minaret
which, in the still oblique sunlight, has a ruddy bronze tinge.

Farther on, we follow a path bordered for more than a
kilometre by a row of tall date palms, all alone in the emptiness
of the valley. Under their moving shade, a subterranean *seguia*
makes an occasional appearance in clear, fresh rivulets.

Kenadsa rises before us, great *ksar* of deep-tinted, warm
brick, flanked on the left by handsome, very green gardens.
The *ksar* descends in a graceful disorder of terraces, following the gentle slope of a knoll. On the right a golden dune,
with its cornice of rock, heaves itself up abruptly.

A *koubba*, very white, shelters the sepulchre of a Muslim
saint – Lella Aicha – from the family of the illustrious Sidi
M'Hammed Ben-Bou-Ziane, founder of Kenadsa and of the
brotherhood of Ziania.

Around the *koubba*, countless graves are scattered in the
sand. They form an obligatory passage to the habitations of
the living. All Saharan towns begin with cemeteries.

We pass near some nondescript lands, we skirt all the
human dust accumulated there over centuries of abandon-
ment and oblivion, and take the road which outlines the
rampart of the *ksar*. This is a thick, high wall of dark earth,
without battlements, without a chink.

[41]

In a little plaza, some men are lounging, blacks for the most part, who raise themselves slightly to look at us.

You enter the *ksar* by a well-set square gate with heavy double doors, then cross the *Mellah*, the tangy Jewish quarter, its inhabitants holed up in narrow shops along the street.

Here, under the influence of Figuig, Jewesses who wear the same costume otherwise are not cloistered. They chatter, cook, even wash themselves in front of their doors.

We turn again and here we are in another, narrower street – cleaner, too – which ends far beyond us in stark chiaroscuro, under a vault of houses.

Entrance to the Zawiya

What is our goal, what shaded retreat, intended for meditation, rest, dreaming, or forgetfulness? I love these alleys which lead who knows where. Following them I always feel something's about to happen in my life.

The slave has stopped, taken my horse by the bridle, and signalled me to dismount. We pass through one last gate and are in the *zawiya*.

The Ziania *marabouts*, or holy men, have a reputation for being friendly to France. They are peaceful, humane people who welcome any force for justice, demonstrating daily their deference to and respect for facts and plain speaking.

Kenadsa is situated outside the frontier and recognizes the sovereignty of the Sultan of Fez. Here we are, then, in Moroccan territory, 25 kilometres from Bechar, which is French. Where, really, is the border? Where does Algeria end and Morocco begin? Nobody bothers to find out. But what good is a border which is knowingly unspecified? The present situation, hybrid and vague, agrees with the Arab character:

it hurts no one and, so, should please everyone.

Three or four black slaves receive us. My guide repeats to them what Kaddour ou Barka told him: I am Si Mahmoud ould Ali, young Tunisian scholar who is travelling from *zawiya* to *zawiya* for instruction. They seat me then on a sack of folded wool on the ground, while someone notifies the present *marabout*, Sidi Brahim ould Mohammed, to whom I have brought a letter of introduction from one of his brethren in Ain Sefra.

Lined up against the wall, the slaves wait, mutely. Two of them are Kharatines. Young, beardless, they wear the grey *djellaba* of Moroccans and a veil of white muslin around their shaved heads. The third, blacker, taller, in white clothing, is Sudanese, and his face carries the deep scars of a brand. All three are armed with the *koumia*, a long dagger with curved blade, sheathed in tooled leather; its handsome cord of colourful, silken strands is passed through a shoulder-strap.

Finally, after a good quarter-hour's wait, a big black slave, freakishly fat, with little, lively eyes, round and prying, comes up and respectfully kisses the strings of my turban. He conducts me into a vast courtyard, silent and bare.

I was already breathing an atmosphere so peaceful as to be slightly disquieting. This succession of gates closing behind me added to the distance I had just travelled. One more little low door, and we enter into a large, square room resembling the interior of a mosque. The lengthening daylight is diffused through a rectangular opening in the beamed ceiling; rugs are spread; I am *chez moi*. It is here that I will live . . . for how long, God knows.

While the negroes go to fetch some coffee and fresh water for me, my eyes adjust to the dimness and I examine my lodgings – not least from the point of view of security. A stairway, narrow and steep, of black stone, leads to the terrace. To the left, a deep recess furnished with an iron brazier for preparing tea and whose smoke escapes by a hole in the ceiling. In the middle of the room, a little square basin and, at its side, a clay pitcher full of water: the necessities for washing. The still water in the basin can serve as a mirror. Four columns, built into the walls, support the ceiling. At the far end of the room is a wooden door, its painted panels depicting primitive flowers in dull colours.

This guest room must be very old, for the plaster of the walls and beams of the ceiling has acquired a green-black tint. The columns, high as a man, are lovely and shining, as if polished by the friction of hands and clothing.

As have so many other travellers, I will doze in this retreat.

New Life

I was about to close my eyes when Sidi Brahim, the *marabout* of Kenadsa, entered. He stands before me, a corpulent man, his face scarred from smallpox, with a collar of greying beard. His gestures are slow and deliberate, his smile engaging and friendly. Nothing shy about him. He wears very simple, very white clothing under a thin *haik* of wool. A fat, round turban crowns him, without a veil to frame his face. His type is a mixture of the town-dwelling Moroccans, whose lisping accent he shares, and the southern villagers.

Si Mohammed Laredj, his nephew and confidant, accompanies Sidi Brahim. Smaller, thin under his snow-white veils, he also has a pleasant face, an almost timid smile, but eyes intelligent and deep, and very kind.

With great dignity Sidi Brahim welcomes me, then questions me in a discreet tone of voice punctuated by silences and repeated courtesies. The *marabouts* retire in an instant, like white phantoms.

Our interview was brief, yet it left me with an impression of security. I am the guest of these men. I will live in the silence of their house. Already I have caught all the calm of their spirit, peace has penetrated my soul's labyrinth. Days to come will pass over me, long and undisturbed, and my curiosity will grow mild as a nurse in a convalescent's room. I will delve into the secrets of my tumultuous psyche. The burning issues of the intellect and the emotions will be reduced to cinders; I will be able to breathe my life with a measured breath. Is this, then, what I have come to seek? Will all my thirst finally be quenched, and for how long?

The thought of this nirvana already softens my heart: the desert I have crossed was that of my desires. But when my will reawakens, I fear it will want anew, and that I will fail to recall past sufferings. I dream of a sleep which will be a death, and from which I'll awaken armed, strong in a personality regenerated by forgetfulness – of itself.

Embarek climbs up to the terrace and throws a mat over the 'eye of the house'. Then, in the darkness, the swarms of flies which were assailing me vanish. A little freshness, a breath of air comes to me from above, with an immense silence that feels eternal. I lie down on the rug in my solitude and pass little by little from calm repose to the oppressive sleep of a siesta.

Slaves

To be always surrounded by black faces, to see them every day anew, to hear only the shrill voices of slaves, with their drawling accents: this is my first impression of daily life at Kenadsa.

Apart from some rare Berber families, all the inhabitants of the *ksar* are black Kharatines. At the *zawiya*, the Sudanese element adds further to my feeling of dislocation.

Sons of captives taken by the Souah and the Mossi tribes, the fathers of these slaves came to Kenadsa after years of suffering and complicated wanderings. Captured first by men of their own race during the constant warring between villages and black chieftains, they were sold to Moorish traffickers, then placed in the hands of the Tuareg or the Chaamba who, in their turn, passed them on to the Berbers.

Their children have not retained the language of their homeland, which only a few old people still understand. At Kenadsa, everyone speaks Arabic. The Berber dialect, Chella, so widespread on the Moroccan frontier, is unknown here.

The Sudanese of the *zawiya*, to the extent their pedigree remains pure, are robust and often handsome, with a completely Arab type of beauty, which contrasts sharply with the ebony black of their skin. Those who are offspring of marriages with Kharatines are, in contrast, often puny and ugly, with angular faces and skinny, ill-proportioned limbs.

I find the blacks to be disconcerting and repulsive, mainly because of the extreme mobility of their faces: their ferret's eyes, and features plagued by tics and grimaces. They bring out in me a stubborn sense of their non-humanity, a lack of kinship which I succumb to childishly, every time, in the face of these blacks, my brothers.

There's only one among the slaves that I find likeable: the gatekeeper Ba Mahmadou ou Salem, confidant of Sidi Brahim. He's a tall, tranquil Sudanese, with a face scarred by brands. He wears immaculately white clothes under a long black burnous. In his expressions, his gestures, and in his regular features, there's nothing of the ape-man, grimacing and crafty; or of the animal cunning which passes for intelligence among the blacks.

Ba Mahmadou is conspicuous among the other negroes. He has discovered within himself, or in his slave culture, the secret of deliberate gestures and respectful attitudes, without displaying any of the depressing servility one might expect from a slave. He puts nobility into his greetings – whereas most other negroes don't even know the formula for a proper greeting.

Every time Ba Mahmadou presents himself before white Muslims, he begins by bowing three times in front of them and only approaches barefoot, leaving his worn slippers at the door. However, his respectfulness in no way diminishes him.

It would be a very interesting study to write about the slaves who live here. For this attempt I should have no prejudices in either direction; it should be a natural history as well as a social history. I should first have to be cured of my prejudices about superior races, and my superstitions about inferior ones.

Almost all the slaves possess houses in the *ksar*, gardens in the palm groves, even small flocks. They sell wool, meat, and dates for their own profit, but they remain constrained to work for their masters.

In order to marry they must ask permission of the chief of the *zawiya*, but they are masters in their own homes. They lead, therefore, a double life: of men almost free outside, but slaves within the *zawiya* where their functions are, moreover, defined rather vaguely.

The Little World of Women

Women here comprise a little world apart with its own hierarchy. First of all, Lella (Madame), the mother of Sidi Brahim, has charge of all the interior administration: expenses, receipts, alms. One never sees her, but her power is felt everywhere. Feared and venerated by all, this elderly Muslim queen-mother lives here nearly cloistered, only coming out rarely and heavily veiled in order to visit the tombs of Sidi Ben-Bou-Ziane, and of Sidi Mohammed, her husband.

Around her gravitates a little world of pale women, who are the wives of the *marabouts*. Lower down, there's the community of negresses, virgins, wives, widows, and divorcées.

The coloured women's morals are extremely loose. For a few sous, for a scarf, and even for pleasure, they give themselves to whomever, Arab or negro. They make open advances to guests, offering themselves with casual forwardness which is often funny to watch.

The male slaves manage to contain somewhat the urgings of their blood, but all of black womanhood abandon themselves to instinct, and their quarrels are as frivolous as their loves. Sometimes in the courtyards noisy arguments break out, degenerating into fist fights and naked brawls in the sun.

One morning, two negresses were cursing each other in front of my door:

— Jew's whore!

— Traitor! Thief! Rotten cunt!

— God damn you, Jew, jackal face!

Suddenly, the hissing voice of Kaddour, the steward, came to hush the scandal. The women separated, like snarling bitches, their teeth glittering with insults, and gnawing on words like flesh.

Transformation

It's been more than a week since I came here, and my life flows smoothly, like a lazy stream. Up to now, I've not left the *zawiya*. You wouldn't dream of doing anything here

[48]

without the authorization of Sidi Brahim. You'd run up against the slaves' silence and the firmly shut doors.

Why wouldn't I be allowed to leave? This question was becoming oppressive and worrying. My precious solitude was no longer voluntary; my room, so conducive to interior visions, was closing in on me like a prison cell.

Finally, this morning, I asked to see the *marabout* and told him my desire. He smiled.

'Si Mahmoud, my child, don't poison your thoughts! If you would like to leave, nothing prevents you. Only, if you do, you must change your costume. You know, the Algerian one you wear is not well regarded here. It doesn't present any real danger to you, but it would surely bring you occasions for distress – you would be treated openly as a *M'zani.*'

Basically, the Moroccans abhor Algerians, whom they consider absolute renegades. Moroccans may detest Algerian Muslims more deeply even than Christians, for they see the former as having abjured Islam, while the latter remain what they've always been: infidels. Forgetting the principles of tolerance propounded by Islam at its purest, the Moroccans harbour an irreconcilable hatred for Christians and *M'zanat.*

So here I am, in order to go out, transforming myself into a Moroccan, discarding the heavy trappings of Algerian horsemen for the light, white *djellaba*, yellow slippers on bare feet, and the little white, veilless turban, rolled into a halo around a *chechiya*. It is lighter and cooler but, fearful of the terrible midday sun, I ask Ba Mahmadou if this nearly transparent head covering will be sufficient to protect me. The Sudanese smiles calmly:

'God and Sidi Brahim Ben-Bou-Ziane will protect you, if you have come here with confidence and sincerity!'

Let's hope that Ba Mahmadou's reassuring prediction will prove true, and that this new costume, which I'm enjoying for the moment, will not call into question my soul's sincerity.

* * *

[49]

The 'Barga' is this strange dune dominating Kenadsa, crowned by blocks of stone with scattered spurs of rock to form a pyramid. I go there for a walk one clear, fresh morning, crossing the cemeteries. Behind the *koubba* of Lella Aicha, blushing pink in the morning light, I climb by a sandy path meandering under the frieze of stones that seem ready to roll into the chasm.

The distance lengthens in an infinite series of transparencies. At the horizon, towards the east, Djebel Bechar rises, very blue, commanding all the landscape from Ben Zireg to Kenadsa.

The sun climbs slowly. It swims in an ocean of carmine rays which dissolve into the green-gold of the zenith. I think about the canvases of Noiré, the only painter who has understood all the delicacy of southern mornings.

Everything here sings with colour, is gradually animated by the sun's fervour. The sand goldens and the stones glow, iridescent. Green, orange, and red reflections bring forth gardens of light on the dryness of this hill. The light is alive on it, becoming my dream palette.

And behind this marvellous screen, there is still more. First, a valley narrow as a ravine. I have walked there, my foot has raked the scaly black stone, like walking on a snake's skin, making me shiver. Beyond that come the salty *sebkhas*, intersected by dark palm groves; then the dunes become a tangled confusion, and you know that's the route of the wadi Guir.

When I climb my little mountain of light, I see the good life, in full colour, spread at my feet. The *ksar* seems to be made for my eyes; I love the warmth and depth of its hue, containing both dark violet and red-brown. At the newer walls the earth is still shaded with flat gold or silvered chamois, like the sand of the dunes. Two or three high houses with latticed windows, those of the *marabouts*, rise above the chaos of the humbler village dwellings.

At the far end of the *ksar*, in the middle of a sort of plaza where there are some tombs, stands the *koubba* of Lella Keltoum (another saint descended from Sidi Ben-Bou-Ziane). I would like to be able to climb this Muslim *koubba*, but it is only a cube of earth. It is very old, and at its angles are ornaments in the shape of pointed horns. From the middle of its terrace rises a little eight-sided cupola. A woman in faded pink *mlahfa*, doubtless a beggar, is seated on the threshold. The cream-coloured minaret, burnished by time and sun, points towards the yellow ball on high. A few members of the Ouled Djerir tribe, ragged and armed with rifles, travel towards the Guir, driving before them about twenty bald camels, loaded with long, black woollen sacks full of grain.

On to this plaza descends the eternal hour, the hour that sparked at the dawning of the world; the hour when, some 200 years ago, the blessed sheikh M'Hammed proclaimed here his humanitarian and esoteric doctrines.

The Enlightened One

At the summit of the Barga, in the middle of a pile of dark rocks, a hermit lives at the back of a narrow cell carved out of the stone.

Dressed in sombre rags, his body lean and tall, his fine face bronzed and emaciated, the anchorite has let his grey hair and unkempt beard grow long. His expression has become fixed, and his lips unceasingly murmur the same mystic invocations which have maintained in him, these twenty years, a state of constant ecstasy.

In his youth, before the grace of unknowing had touched him, this enlightened one travelled widely – in Morocco, in

Algeria, in the desert and in the Sudan. This must have been one of those admirable journeys which, in our day, only Arabs still know how to make, going on foot from village to village asking for shelter and bread, on the path of God.

Then, tired of the vanity of human knowledge and of the world's monotony, the saint returned to his native land and retired forever into his grey cell from which he would never-more venture, except to be carried by believers towards the definitive calm of the hazy necropolis below.

I watch him, this good Saharan anchorite, and I think that the Christian hermits of the first centuries must have re-sembled him, amidst their similarly desolate scenery – scorching Thebes and Cyrene. They too sought through ecstasy to satisfy the imperious need for eternity, a need which slumbers deep in all simple souls.

I experience this need myself at times . . . not always. Others have told me that they never suffer from it, and they were not just crude rationalists; they aspired to life, to all of life, as to a burst of illumination that must be followed by eternal night. One of them, with whom I have shared the purest of my soul's dreams, in a few minutes of exaltation and nostalgia said to me: 'I find no savour in life except in the certainty of dying one day. I need to know that this will not last.' This state of mind astonished me.

Perhaps the hermit of Barga resides in eternity.

The Marabout's Indignation

Yesterday during the siesta, Sidi Brahim entered suddenly, holding a letter in his hand, and clearly dismayed.

'Si Mahmoud, I have just received a letter from Oujda, which says that Hadj Mohammed ould Abdelkhaut, chief of the Kadriya, has been assassinated by Bou Amama's people – may God punish them!'

And the *marabout* dropped on to the rug, handing me the letter. It was written on a bit of grey paper, all crumpled, and delivered by a messenger from the *zawiya* of Oujda, here to the *zawiya* of the Zianias, across 250 miles.

The messenger recounted the death of Hadj Mohammed, who had visited Bou Amama to persuade him not to bring desolation and war into Angad.

Bou Amama received the emissary well and showered him with promises. But, as Hadj Mohammed returned over the plain, one of Bou Amama's men caught up with him. Under the pretext of having a secret communication for him, the agent led Hadj Mohammed apart from his companions. Then, in the bed of a wadi, the yellow scum murdered the unfortunate *marabout*.

Managing to decipher the nearly illegible scrawl, I imagined Oujda besieged, prey to greedy and inflamed soldiers, a mob trampling the dirt where carcasses lay rotting. And, at the focus of all this terror, behind ruins where pink peach trees flourished, the white, contained *zawiya* of the Kadriyas, from whose calm Hadj Mohammed had ventured, only to be treacherously assassinated. There, barely three months before, I had been welcomed like a brother.

'Si Mahmoud, the Moghreb is lost if out there they begin killing innocent men of prayer and alms, who carry neither sword nor gun,' Sidi Brahim said to me.

'God must have blinded the sons of the Moghreb, for them to have so abandoned his path that they betray their Sultan, descended from the Prophet – prayers and salutation to him! – through Mouley Idris; and to follow whom? Miserable impostors like Bou Amama and the Rogui Bou Hamara!' In his mild, slow voice Sidi Brahim continued to lament over the fate of Morocco.

'How on earth is the popularity of Bou Amama to be ex-

[53]

plained, except by madness? – the son of a notorious junk dealer from Figuig, without background or education, instigator of fighting and killing, dispenser of false miracles and empty promises. Believe me, Bou Amama's house is built on foundations of lies and sin! But the desert nomads are such fools that the greater the improbability, the stronger is their belief! As for anyone who comes telling the truth to them, let him beware: they scorn him and, if they can, they exterminate him.

'Si Mahmoud, you have read the word of God, you have visited many towns and countries, so what do you say of the Rogui? How do you explain the unbelievable fortune of this man whom no one knows and who, overnight, sets himself up as Sultan, emir of the believers? He says that he is Mouley M'hammed, dispossessed brother of Mouley Abdelaziz. But why then can't he find a single trustworthy man among those who have known Mouley M'hammed, to attest to the believers, "It's really he" or else silence the impostor? Some claim that Bou Hamara is the originator of the Sanhadja of Mount Zerhaoun. But why does no one among the Sanhadja and the Beni Zerhaoun know this man? One is tempted to believe that this Bou Hamara is no son of Adam, but a *djinn*, a fire sprite, a sign of the times, a scourge from God, descended from the sky or spawned from the earth to chastise the depraved and criminal Moghreb.

'You easterners are fortunate. You enjoy in peace the goods granted you by the Bestower. But we unhappy sons of the Moghreb live in a country of ravening wolves, where the rivers overflow with blood and where wickedness triumphs. At each hour of the day and night we tremble for our lives and for our property.

'Look, Si Mahmoud, we had important revenues in Tafilala, at El Outtat, at Fez and above all in the region of the Angad. At present, since the impostors' armies have invaded the country, we receive only a quarter of those revenues. And here the poor, the orphans, unprotected women, students, and travellers abound, asking us for asylum and bread, which we must give them according to the rule of our master – may God reward him! – Ah, Si Mahmoud, let us pray God to annihilate Bou Amama, son of the junk dealer, inventor of lies, and Bou Hamara, that devil who, riding a she-ass, aspires to a millenarian throne, to negate the legacy Mouley Idris has left his posterity by the will of the Inheritor of Worlds.'

And so, every day, Sidi Brahim comes to inform me of news from the west, sad news, and of rumours from outside. But the echoes of torment rumbling across rotten Morocco carry very faintly into this distant retreat. Here nothing happens, and news from the outside world, entering Kenadsa's warmth and purity, fails to infect it with tragedy's icy shiver.

In the monotony of my life here I lose little by little my habits of agitation and unchained passions. Surely everywhere, as here, the course of events has run down.

A Message

A long day spent in fever and pain, heavy hours passed in the small terrace room, bedded on a mat, facing the fiery horizon.

In the evening, as the air freshened a little, I felt better and got up to go out to the parapet: one of my favourite sensations, which I find voluptuously mellow, is to encounter the sunset over Kenadsa, aureoled in royal purple.

The slaves are late in coming today. Night falls, a night moonlit and perfectly transparent.

Still nothing: neither tea, nor dinner, and only a little water left at the bottom of the leather *delloua*, dripping slowly. I call. On an adjoining terrace, an old negress appears out of the shadows: the slaves have all gone to a wake in the neighbourhood of the mosque.

So I arrange my rug as well as possible on the still-warm terrace and go to bed in the pink light of the moon descending toward the horizon.

Near dawn, Ba Mahmadou comes to me contritely, and greets me even more respectfully than usual:

'Sidi Mahmoud, "Lella" sends me to say that she begs you, in the name of God and of Sidi Ben-Bou-Ziane, to pardon her and to drive from your heart all bitterness. Yesterday evening we all accompanied her to the deathbed of a holy woman, Lella Fathima Angadia, who died at the hour of *moghreb* – God have mercy on her! – This is why "Lella" forgot to send you tea and the evening meal. She asks you to pardon this involuntary offence and calls upon you the blessing of God and her ancestors.'

I never see this 'Lella', all-powerful, so venerated, who upholds the cult of hospitality to the point of sending this stranger a message stamped with such gentle humility, to beg pardon for an inconsequential lapse.

What is she like, this great Muslim lady, whose presence I can never enter as Si Mahmoud, the man whom everyone treats me as being? – Even if, due to indiscretions at Bechar, they have suspicions, they carefully avoid letting me know, for this would be a grave breach of Muslim courtesy.

Does she have the serious manner of Sidi Brahim? And what thoughts occupy the head of this woman so specially placed: cloistered, yet invested with an authority before which her son himself yields?

Vision of Women

Rays the colour of red copper gleamed obliquely on the tawny brick walls of the large courtyard. I was seated on a rock, waiting for Sidi Brahim. As every evening, the women were coming to the fountain, and I watched their slow procession and the splendour of their clothing in the light.

There were young and old, beautiful and ugly; and others went by, their heads bent, anonymous except for their barely murmured greeting.

Under the low vault of the door which opens on to the interior court, two young women had paused. One was a Sudanese negress with a round face and large, russet doe's eyes. Small but weighty chains of silver passed through her earlobes and dangled down to her shoulders; silver snakes fastened the two long mats of her jet-black hair that spread across her chest.

A citron-yellow *mlahfa* was wound in soft folds round her tall, thin body. Seated, her elbows on her knees, she was speaking with expressive hand gestures, her palms waving and bracelets clicking.

The other, a mulatta, remained standing. Her strange beauty was alluring; an aquiline profile, dark and fine; large, sad eyes; voluptuous, arched lips revealing fine teeth.

A *mlahfa* of red wool, the hue of pale blood, draped her supple form. One of the panels of her veils fell straight down from her head to her arching loins, passing behind her lovely nude arm, the colour of old bronze. She held herself very straight, with her large, terracotta amphora resting on her rounded hip.

The mulatta listened to her companion gravely, without smiling.

A light breeze stirred their veils, spreading a penetrating odour of peppered cinnamon and of moist black flesh. Against the rosy grey background of the wall, the two women stayed a long time conversing in the violet light of evening, which was darkening little by little under the archway of the door.

They appeared very beautiful to me like that, set in this corner of the courtyard: two African women whose clothing was alive.

[57]

Friday Prayer

Today, Friday, a trip to the mosque for the public prayer. A little after noon, in the oppression and silence of the siesta, from very far, as in a dream, a drawling voice reaches me: it's the *zoual*, the first call.

I rise and with a cold bath try to dispel my drowsiness. Then, following Farradji, a taciturn Sudanese, I venture into the blinding glare of the courtyard. Instinctively we keep close to the walls, our feet on the ribbon of shade which borders them. We follow the narrow lanes, the crumbling garden walls, and find ourselves in the valley of sand.

Everything burns and glitters with metallic reflections, from the dry stones of the Barga to the salty sand of the *sebkhas* where heat waves sketch vague mirages. It is the deadly hour of sunstroke and fever, the hour when you feel crushed, pulverized, chest on fire, head empty.

Finally we arrive, entering the *ksar* where a little shade persists. Several forms precede us; we follow, a wordless crowd, led by the same thought. Where the worshippers pass, blind beggars chant their supplication. We have to climb over the mosque's enclosure, barred to prevent children and beasts from entering. Here, with the same gesture, all the Muslims take off their yellow slippers and carry them in their hands. In our turn we cross the courtyard, barefoot, almost running, to escape the intolerable burning of the overheated sand.

As soon as we enter the sanctuary, there's a delicious feeling of refreshment, of dim light, of infinite peace. Everything is bare and white in this extremely old Saharan refuge: the walls, and the heavy pillars, sturdy and standing in pairs which, with old rough beams of date wood, support the ceiling. Filtered, diffuse daylight falls from above through small openings, making blue and yellow tracks and leaving all the depth of the mosque in shadow. On worn mats, the people of Kenadsa and the nomads pray. To the right, under a larger, dormer window, bathed in warmer light, the *talebs*, students and professors of the *medersa*, chant the Koran. Behind them, school children repeat the lessons of their elders.

Here and there, kneeling near a pillar, an isolated *taleb* recites aloud the litanies of the Prophet.

And all these voices – the serious voices of men, some very pure and beautiful which dominate the others, and the clear voices of children – combine in a great, confused murmur, following a monotonous and melancholy air, falling to a finale with each phrase.

How it creeps along and then climbs; and what a feeling of duration it embodies, this lulling chant in the echoing nave!

Then, suddenly, up there on the minaret, the *mueddin* cries out his second call. His voice seems to descend from unknown spheres, simply because he is very high and invisible. And here, in our communion of mind, we are constantly on the brink of the marvellous.

At the conclusion of the last verse, the *talebs'* voices sustain the last note and are extinguished in a sigh; and immediately, with a noisy clatter, the children get up and run out, lightening the ponderous air of mystery with their naïvety and lively joy.

Everything's silent now, all heads bent attentively.

From the dark depths of the *mihrab*, the large niche indicating the direction of Mecca, the broken and tremulous voice of the *imam* rises. He reads the *Khotba*, the long prayer mixed with exhortations, that takes the place of a sermon and which we listen to seated and in silence.

The *imam* is not at all a priest – it's well known that Islam has no regular clergy – he is simply the most learned, the most venerated *taleb* in the congregation. Any learned man may serve as *imam*: he must simply recite the prayer.

In Islam there are no mysteries, no sacraments, nothing which requires the mediation of a priest.

[59]

During the *Khotba*, a few more moments of reverie, of great, sweet peace.

A man in a white shirt belted with a simple cord, bareheaded, carries a skin of fresh water and a clay cup: he provides refreshment to old and sick people. It's a good work that he takes on himself thus, every Friday.

A final call from the *mueddin*, and the old *imam* finishes his reading and begins to pray.

A young man with a strong and sonorous voice is placed near him and repeats the invocations in a sort of plainchant.

All the assembly stand, our hands in front of our faces, then our arms fall alongside our bodies, and the people repeat with the *imam* and the chanter: 'Allahou Akbar!' – God is great.

We bend and prostrate ourselves.

The prayer ended, I remain with the *talebs* and the *marabouts*, who recite again the rhymed litanies of the Prophet.

'Prayer and peace be upon you, O Mohammed, Prophet of God, you the greatest of creatures now and forever, in heaven and on earth . . . Prayer and peace be upon you, O Mohammed the Chosen, Arab prophet, a torch in the darkness, the key to our faith, O Mohammed of the Koreish, master of Mecca and of flowering Medina, lord of Muslim men and women, now and forever. . . .'

The *marabouts* have beautiful deep voices. They know the old melody which so nobly carries the ringing verses of this litany, which the common folk just recite very quickly, in a nasal, staccato voice.

It is over. We rise and each one takes up his slippers from his mat and places one on top of the other.

One more time, we have to cross the blinding furnace of the valley.

My courage falters and I ask Farradji to lead me through the *ksar*'s maze of black tunnels, so low that you have to bend double for more than a hundred metres. The darkness is

[60]

opaque in these bowels, and the going rough, but here reigns the ancient dankness of a cave.

Following on the calm of the last hour passed in the mosque's blue shade, this return is a nightmare.

It strikes me that prayer, and dreams, too, should never end.

Lella Khaddoudja

Ba Mahmadou daydreams on the steps of the staircase while the water for tea sings in the kettle. He looks round the room and at the simple paintings on the door, at the back.

'I wonder where the mistress of this house is, at this moment!' he says with a sigh.

I ask whom he means, and the Sudanese tells me that this house belongs to one Lella Khaddoudja, a relative of Sidi Brahim. Being widowed very young, with two children, a boy and a little girl, the pious *maraboute* remarried one of her cousins on the strict condition that they leave immediately for Mecca. The cousin kept his promise, and Lella Khaddoudja left the *zawiya*, leaving her son behind.

'The day she left Kenadsa,' says Ba Mahmadou, 'we all, every servant, accompanied her as far as the Ain ech Cheikh fountain, on the road to Bechar. From her seat on muleback she turned one last time to look at the *ksar*, and told us she would never return, because she would rather live and die on the sacred soil of Hedjaz. This winter it will be two years since she left. She wrote to her brother once, to tell him that she arrived too late for the Jedda pilgrimage and that she was waiting at Jerusalem for this year's, after which she would settle for good in one of the two holy towns. God grant her aid and mercy! She was a holy woman, and kind toward all us poor slaves!'

[61]

I, too, begin musing about Lella Khaddoudja, who must have a rather adventurous soul, to break so willingly with the sleepy routine, the cloistered life she was born to, to go off and start a new life under another sky.

What occurred in the heart of this travelling holy woman? What caused her swift resolution to leave forever her native *ksar*? What was the romance of her solitary soul? . . . a romance that no one will write; that no one will know.

'Such is life,' concludes Ba Mahmadou. 'We knew Lella Khaddoudja, we saw her every day, we sought her help, and now she is far, so far away. And we'll never see her again. *Voila*!'

I realize that for the unlettered Sudanese, Jerusalem and the towns of Syria and Arabia lie at the farthest ends of the earth. They must seem to him cities of dream, almost imaginary.

Nomad Lords

At five o'clock in the evening I'm under the white arches of the *riad* – the large portico which extends over the interior garden in Sidi Brahim's house. Outside, in the valley, the sirocco raises dust storms, but here there is only a light breeze to dissipate the heaviness in the last heat of day. On a large, brightly coloured rug from Rabat, Sidi Brahim half reclines, leaning on a silk cushion embroidered with golden olives. One by one, Smain's ebony prayer-beads click; seated against the wall, Si Mohammed Laredj pours onto a square of scarlet silk two sacks of Spanish *douros*, tarnished from the silos' dampness.

Before him, squatting in a half-circle, are three chiefs of the Doui Menia from the Guir river. One of them, very old, his face cut with deep wrinkles, tanned by the sun to the colour of earth, his white beard stiff and bristly, is wrapped in an old *haik* of light wool, with a hilted *koumia* and copper sheath.

The second, also old, is rolled up in a worn burnous. He hides his weapons under his veils and assumes a solemn attitude, out of keeping with his coarse manners and his rapacious profile, a long nose hooked over a toothless mouth. He is a representative of the Zianias from Guir.

The third, the youngest and most important of the three, might be thirty-five. He is tall, muscular, and wears white under a heavy burnous of black camel skin. His damascened *koumia* with its gilded hilt is held by a thick cord of violet silk slung crosswise over his shoulder. An orange cord supports a red leather satchel, gold-embroidered, from Fez. He also carries a magnificent revolver with an engraved silver butt. He is barefoot, though, having left his sandals, his archaic nomad's *naala*, near the door.

His bronzed face is intelligent and evasive, with a refined expression; an energetic face framed by a strong black beard. This sheikh Embarek would be handsome if his wolf's teeth did not extend so far past his lip, making his face, when he speaks, look cruel and repugnant.

Embarek exercises great influence over the Ouled Bou Anane, and he is plotting for absolute leadership of his tribe. Since the Ouled Bou Anane have made peace with the French, and frequent the markets south of Oran, Embarek foresees the complete annexation. He is ready to assist this, for he hopes by then to be the great chief of all the Doui Menia: he to whom Christians 'would give a scarlet burnous and decorations!' Embarek is ambitious and smart, but he is also a gunpowder man, a highwayman, having only renounced the traditional pillaging in hope of extracting greater profit from peace than from skirmishes.

Sidi Brahim wants to entrust these nomad chiefs with important purchases of sheep on the Guir river. They are returning there from Beni Ounif, where they have furnished camels for a caravan. It is the price of sheep that Si Moham-med Laredj is in the process of reckoning, accompanied by pleasantries and his gentle manners.

The Doui Menias' greedy eyes devour the *douros* as they clatter into a heap. Instinctively they move closer, leaning towards this money which will soon be theirs. For they are sure to find traders who will name as high a price as possible.

They pretend not to know how to count and constantly interrupt, confusing Si Mohammed's calculations. Then, seeing that this could go on indefinitely, Sidi Brahim asks me to write down the figures. Kneeling, I scribble with a reed, in 'Indian' numbers used by Arabs, so that Embarek, who knows how to read, may verify them.

Finally, the nomads surrender to the evidence. The old schemers already stretch their bony hands towards the money, but Embarek has not spoken his last. He stops the others with a gesture.

'Sidi Brahim,' he says with his most engaging smile, 'the count is correct: 650 *douros* are needed to pay for the sheep at today's price, and the money is there. Certainly, we are your servants, and servants of your glorious grandfather, Sidi Ben-Bou-Ziane – God grant him his favours! But we must look for the sheep among our brothers scattered over the course of the Guir. Then we must drive them all the way back here, so that the Ouled Nasr tribe and the Ait Khebbach Berbers don't steal them. We take responsibility for all this, and are truly happy to serve you. You have nothing to fear – God willing! But we are poor nomads ruined by war, and surely your generosity will not forget this. Give us some recompense for our trouble.'

Sidi Brahim smiles. Si Mohammed Laredj lowers his head and assumes an impenetrable expression.

'And what recompense do you wish?'

'Give us two hundred French francs, and God return your beneficence.'

'Pray to the prophet', answered Sidi Brahim, 'and curse Iblis who interferes with men, sowing hatred among them, and makes them prefer the goods of this world over truth and justice. If this is how it is, and your services must be bought at such a high price, I prefer to send my slaves to the Guir.'

For a good while longer the Doui Menia argue, but the *marabout* accedes nothing more to their greed. While the nomads fume and even dare to raise their voices, Sidi Brahim and Si Mohammed remain silent. They wait.

Finally, seeing the uselessness of their efforts, Embarek and the old men return to mild speech, with forced smiles.

'Sidi Brahim, you are our master, and we don't dare dispute your decisions, for your decrees are final. Remain in peace, and pray for us to God, his Prophet – blessings and peace be upon him – and to Sidi M'Hammed Ben-Bou-Ziane, for tomorrow at dawn we will set off for the Guir.'

'Go in peace, my sons, and God protect you and guide you along the right path.' And the nomads rise, their weapons clattering. They turn once more to look regretfully at the *douros* as Si Mohammed Laredj returns them to their sacks, where they disappear with a tantalizing ring.

Messaoud

For the last few days a black boy named Messaoud has been serving me. He's about 14 years old, tall for his age and too sharp for his own good. He dresses in white shirts pulled in at the waist by a belt of grey wool. His brown face is friendly and expressive, with mischievous, large dark eyes that seem to have no iris. On his shaved head, a little tuft of crisped hair, sign of slavery and also of pre-adolescence, is a comic fixture above his right ear. This bizarre ornament lends a humorous touch to his otherwise mocking features. In the pierced lobe of his ear Messaoud wears a piece of rolled blue paper, in lieu of an earring.

He's nosy and nimble as a cat, a scrounger and liar, and loquacious like all the blacks here. In Messaoud I have a schemer for a slave. When I send him to buy some tobacco from the Jew he runs there fast enough, but on his return he cheats me over the complicated Moroccan change. He can tell I'm at a loss with the confusing coinage used here in the west, and he profits by my ignorance. When I scold him for his conduct, he begins by denying it, swearing pathetically, then ends up bursting into laughter, as if my scolding struck him as very funny.

For a cup of mint tea, he'd do anything. Once that's achieved he becomes deaf to all orders, showing incorrigible sloth and intricate animal cunning. He dares to openly mock the other slaves, his elders, almost everyone – mindless of reprisals.

Ba Mahmadou regards Messaoud with horror: 'He's a black pest, a sinful child, a calamity!' And the porter rolls his big soft eyes, trying to intimidate Messaoud with his gaze, but the boy just laughs and escapes.

When he wants something he can act humble and affectionate, even simperingly good. This exaggerated obligingness becomes tiresome very quickly, but ceases as soon as he gets what he wants. A voracious glutton, he licks the plates and gnaws all day on stolen sugar.

Messaoud loves no one, not even Blal, his elderly father, a humble farmer in Sidi Brahim's fields. When the old man happens to come near the courtyard, Messaoud chases him brutally, with all the scorn of a well-situated domestic for the peasant. To all my reproaches on this point – which interests me, since I have a theory that in many children natural love for their parents is lacking – the little good-for-nothing retorts, grimacing: 'He is dirty! He smells like shit! He is lousy!'

With the *marabouts*, Messaoud is only respectful enough to avoid blows. They scold him; he sticks out his tongue as soon as their backs are turned.

Little animal full of graces and vices; familiar daimon held by all in lowest esteem; this black boy has taught me so much about white children.

Saharan Theocracy

The influence of the Arab *marabouts* has deeply altered the secular institutions and customs of the people of Kenadsa. Among all the other Berbers, it is the *djemaa*, the assembly of factions or of the ksars, that rules. All political or administrative questions are submitted to the *djemaa* for deliberation. Should the body require a chief, the *djemaa* elects him. As long as he remains invested with this authority the chief is obeyed, but he remains accountable to those who have chosen him.

These Berber assemblies are tumultuous. Passions are given free rein; violent, they sometimes end in bloodshed. However, the Berbers always remain jealous of their collective freedoms. They defend themselves against tyranny while supporting those who try to impose it.

At Kenadsa, the Arab theocratic tendency has triumphed over the Berber tradition, which is republican and confederate. The chief of the *zawiya* is the only hereditary lord of the *ksar*. It is he who settles all questions and who, in the case of war, appoints military chiefs. It is he who renders criminal justice, while civil affairs are judged by the *cadi*. Yet here too, the *marabout* is the supreme authority, to whom one may appeal the *cadi*'s decisions.

Sidi M'Hammed Ben-Bou-Ziane, the founder of the

brotherhood, wanted to make of his disciples a pacifist and hospitable association. The *zawiya* extends the right of asylum to every criminal who takes refuge there. Though he is sheltered from human justice, if he is a thief the *marabout* makes him return the stolen goods. If he's an assassin, he must pay the blood price. Aside from these conditions, the guilty incur no other punishment as long as they are within the precincts of the *zawiya* or of some territory belonging to it.

Capital punishment is not applied by the *marabouts*. If it happens that a criminal is put to death, it is by the relatives of the victim or sometimes even by his own; never is he condemned by the *marabouts*. However, these descendants of Sidi Ben-Bou-Ziane are known to be quite severe with thieves and scandalmongers among the villagers or the slaves, and on these they inflict beatings with the Bastinado. Usually, though, at the time of the execution one of the witnesses rises and pleads for the guilty one to be spared. Sometimes it's the women, who send as envoy with this request a slave or a negress. The *marabout* always yields.

Thanks to the *zawiya*, misery is unknown in Kenadsa. No beggars in the streets of the *ksar*; all unfortunates take refuge in the *zawiya*'s protective shadow, and live there as long as they please. Most make themselves useful as servants, workers, or shepherds, but no one is compelled to work.

The maraboutic influence has been so profound at Kenadsa that Berbers and Kharatines have forgotten their dialects and speak nothing but Arabic. Their manners have also been mellowed and refined compared to those of villagers elsewhere. Arguments, especially brawls, are rare, because the people are used to bringing their differences before the *marabouts*, who calm them and impose mutual concessions on them.

Since the *marabouts*' neighbourly rapport and increasing friendship with the French, a secret discontent has invaded the hearts of the lower classes. No one dares raise his voice and criticize the masters' acts. They bow, they repeat the

[68]

opinions of Sidi Brahim and even praise them, but were it not for his enormous moral authority, they would consider him and his disciples to be 'M'zanat' – renegades.

What is the future of Kenadsa, and what will remain in a few years' time of this tiny theocratic state, so unique and so sequestered? Certainly, after the toughness of Figuig and the dark chaos of Oujda, one is truly impressed to find on the desert's edge this tranquil corner, calling itself Moroccan but resembling so little the rest of Morocco.

In the Margin of a Letter

I no longer know one day from the next, only that it is the heart of summer. I have a fever, interrupted by painful, lucid and sensual respites.

Yesterday I received a letter drenched in a different sunlight than this. And so: because you've been smiled upon by new faces, shall you become such an egoist as to hold up this joy to old friends?

When I return to Algiers, that place where my heart capsized, where my desire is no longer anchored, whose golden mornings darken my mourning – of what shall we speak if not of ourselves, and how?

Women cannot understand me, they see me as a freak. I am much too simple for their taste, which is obsessed with the superficial and its artifice. They drivel on, composing an endless comedy, always the same thing. They don't even allow the costumes to change. When woman becomes the comrade of man, when she ceases to be a plaything, she will begin another existence. But for now, they only know how to breathe in time and to the theme of a waltz.

They say a new generation is at hand and that certain

young women now know how to speak without flirting, even at the height of social goings-on. I don't believe it at all; or else it's just another trick of education which will never stand up to the pressure of the salons.

Meanwhile, what will they do for husbands, these sincere young women? since men, especially in the provinces, are still nothing but skirt-chasers. Woman herself will be everything desired, but I've seen no sign that men desire her to change except within the limits of fashion. A slave or an idol, this is what they can love – never an equal.

I've jotted these reflections in the margin of a letter which has come to me from so far, on the winds of cruel thoughtlessness. Having written them, I relapse into my feeling of exile, wishing to bury myself even deeper in this hostile south, without any desire for the Paris I have known, where the newspapers' lip-service to feminism was even more repugnant to me than the Parisian coquettes.

I have said nothing in my response worth reading. Why bother? One day paths separate, destinies crystallize. And this is so much more than having made a few friends. When they are good enough to invite us to share their foreign happiness, let's show them what's possible to a true fraternity of minds.

Let's regret nothing, since our happiness and theirs will consist in letting ourselves go one day into mysterious currents which will carry our souls adrift towards impossible shores. Then we'll enjoy the intoxication of decadence and shipwreck; and wandering over the immense beaches of the night, we'll feel within us the seeds of suffering begin to germinate.

* * *

Garden Meal

In order to distract me, knowing I am ill, Sidi Brahim invites me to a meal outdoors, in the gardens of the *zawiya*. Si Abdel Ouahab, a scholar from the east who's come to settle at Kenadsa, was sent to me with this message.

I admire how the smallest things here take on fullness and nobility. Bluntness and disregard for ceremony are European qualities intended to make life more comfortable. And when one has grown accustomed to this candour from people, it's hard to take seriously the airs which, on certain days, in certain circumstances, the commonest people affect, those least capable of delicacy and feeling. All their politeness rings false; their speech is pretentious, awkward. But here, politeness is not a formula, it is a way of being and is completely sincere: it takes part in characters, it harmonizes with costumes, there is nothing subservient and nothing affected about it. It pleases.

At first, Sidi Brahim's invitation surprises me. In Europe or in the Algerian Tell, no one would dream of organizing a picnic in such weather. The sky is a turbid black; ghastly clouds scud past, almost brushing the tops of dunes. They pass over in shreds and return to pile strangely upon each other, like scraps of unravelling silk. A violent wind chases them, though it's unnoticeable on the ground, where it doesn't even ruffle the tops of the motionless date palms. Heavy warm drops begin to fall.

But it's just this kind of weather that allows expansion and growth. Here in the desert scorched by an eternal thirst, it's a luxury to have this lightly moist air, the sky dimmed and cool. It would take more than this slight rainfall to make my parched skin shiver.

I can hardly drag myself after the ten days of misery I've endured, bedded on a mat, brought to ground by fever. But I accept the invitation.

[71]

The garden is surmounted by the high houses of the *ksar*. The tilled fields rise in tiers gently up to a terrace, where some lovely rugs from Djebel Amour are spread, their high soft pile reflecting dark velvet tones under the dull light of the storm.

Below, the virgin vines climb up the slender trunks of date palms, or wind themselves freely around the grey, twisted branches of fig trees. Two young captive gazelles play, chasing one another under the foliage and leaping the irrigation streams that are choked with golden mint.

Sidi Brahim leans on a cushion. Around him, a few relatives, intimates, and familiars. Here is Taleb Ahmed, the secretary of the *zawiya*: tall and robust, with a strong trace of negro blood showing under his glowing skin. Intelligent and observant, Taleb Ahmed contrasts with the *marabout* in his simple, almost jovial facial expressions.

Si Mohammed, Taleb's predecessor, a true settled Berber with a broad, pale face, and sparse, almost red-brown beard, has been estranged from the master for some time. He's there, too, apparently back in Sidi Brahim's good graces.

Distant, his thoughts elsewhere, yet wearing his gentle, almost timid smile, Sidi Mohammed Laredj remains silent, half-reclining on the rug, tracing its arabesques with his finger. His thoughtful, benevolent expression tells of meditations and detachment, though free of asceticism; his face has a certain artist's objectivity which sees the world as a spectacle.

Quite different is the direct expression of Sidi Embarek, maternal uncle of Sidi Brahim. On his fine bronze face and in his depthless eye may be read passions which brook no obstacles; decisiveness; the proud naïvety of the exemplar Arab, decorative and made for decoration – a type known in Algiers in the antechambers of offices and on the terraces of cafés. He is the absolute head of the family. He has had exploits, one much like the next.

In the garden, the slaves prepare the little low tables, and

[72]

the plates covered with tall funnels woven of brightly coloured straw.

Naturally, the conversation turns to the affairs of Morocco, to the Tafilala, and the detested names of Rogui and Bou Amama are mentioned. But today Sidi Brahim has received no bad news, and everyone is jovial. Amusing anecdotes are recounted with the absolute purity of language which well-born Muslims observe in public, and especially among relations.

In the date trees, rinsed of their shroud of dust and turning blue under the morose sky, a whole flock of swallows has been roused to a chorus of sharp, short cries.

'Here we have the *djemaa* of the birds,' says Taleb Ahmed. 'They gather here to conduct the business of their tribe and to make important decisions. These little animals, hardly bigger than flies, make as much racket as one hundred Doui Menia, all debating at the same time.' And the sedate *marabouts* laugh at this critique of their restless neighbours.

The tame gazelles begin playing with the guests, drawing near with a series of complicated feints, only to bound swiftly away.

After the meal with unleavened bread, so fragrant and flavoured with aniseed, there is tea – the eternal tea which Sidi Embarek carefully prepares, with ceremonial motions. Here, to make tea is a task worthy of man, of a free man.

At the end of the grey day we leave, as the hour approaches for the *moghreb* prayer. In the shadow of the *ksar*, the *marabouts* disperse, exchanging slow salutations.

I bring away with me the remembrance of this oriental repast on the garden terrace. I think of all the generations of Kenadsa's *marabouts* who came there on dark days. They must have felt the same pleasure, the same sensations, spoken much the same words. Again I have the sense of immobility, of beings and of things, that the old cities of Islam bring about in me. For a few moments everything endures, everything is eternal.

The Rebel

Today, after the Friday prayer, I find the *ksar* all in a ferment: a young, white Muslim woman has hanged herself. I mingle with the crowd stationed at her house, from which rise the women's lamentations.

I make enquiries and reconstruct the drama, seeking to penetrate her reasons. She was not on good terms with her relatives, I'm told; she had no one to complain to. Her husband, Hammou Hassine, didn't pay attention to her, except to beat her into submission. The little Bedouin, wild at heart, became resigned after a few attempts at revolt, or so it appeared. In actuality a feeling of extraordinary freedom possessed her.

Many times she had fled to her brother, who always returned her to her husband. She was prevented from going to ask protection of the *cadi* or of Sidi Brahim. She was a slave, more slave than the negresses, in that her servitude brought her suffering. At the end she was calm, for she had grasped the key to ultimate liberation. One evening when everyone was at the mosque she mustered her resources for the escape, she raised herself on her little feet, she hung herself above her life and her condition with her long silk belt, without confiding a word to anyone, all by herself.

A people for whom suicide is still possible is a strong people. Animals never kill themselves; nor negroes unless, that is, they are stimulated by alcohol. Suicide is a kind of drunkenness, but a deliberate drunkenness.

The deadened crowd pull back in horror from her, who

neglected her duty to live. However, the scholars have taken pity on Embarka and come to pray over her corpse, which the matrons have washed and sewn into the egalitarian, Islamic shroud. The body is laid on a mat in the middle of the courtyard. It is no more than a vague, rigid form, immaculate. The women's lamentations have ceased. Nothing more to be heard but the recitation of some men who chant, in slow cadence, the chapter of the Koran entitled 'Ya Sine', which is the prayer for the dead.

The courtyard has grown calm, solemn, serene, now that the noisy women have retired.

The voices are raised in a sad, sweet song: it's the 'Borda' this time, the burial elegy. The body is placed on a stretcher of rough wood and covered with a large red veil. Again a moment of silence and attention, then four men load the small body on to their shoulders, and the sad cortège goes off toward the cemetery.

They place the stretcher on the sand and arrange themselves in a semi-circle, facing Mecca: this is the final prayer for Embarka. On the mound of sand which is already being scattered by the wind, they plant three palms which will dry out and die before long. Hammou Hassine, a gross, ugly, and deformed man, arranges a red cotton handkerchief on the ground, and on it places some dried figs and unleavened, flat loaves: these are the ritual alms for the poor in memory of the departed, and which take the place of useless bouquets and gaudy wreaths.

It's over. We leave, in confusion. The old scholars, in their rigour, have kept apart from the suicide's funeral procession. Only the young scholars have prayed for her, because youth divines things that most men forget in their maturity.

How rare are those who can keep developing over a long time! Thought quickly leads to a cessation of growth.

One of them said to me, 'She was unhappy!' He probably had no idea what unhappiness means. The idea of suffering makes men hard. They exchange compassion for condemnation. While it seems to me the heart must open itself – ever more and more.

Then there are those wise men who have kept the desire to learn up to their dying day. Why is it that what we hold true for the intellect, we discount when it comes to educating our hearts? Since I've been living in this *zawiya*, in the shadow of Islam, since my fever and voluntary solitude, I have been horrified by certain hours in my turbulent past; my sensibilities have become more refined. After this retreat, if I return to the passing life, I will have a new understanding of love.

Sudanese Festival

It's four o'clock and the sirocco finally abates, abruptly. Little by little the dust disperses as a light breeze blows from the east. One can breathe again. Doors slam. Villagers and *marabouts* appear in the streets where the wind has laid a shroud of fine sand. In the sky, grey clouds drag again upon the enflamed horizon.

A noise rises in the *ksar*, a sort of rhythmic hammering, rumbling and slowly drawing nearer. It's the Sudanese drums advancing. Their bizarre sound introduces a hint of a more distant Africa into Kenadsa's Saharan setting.

Through the centuries of Islam, the Sudanese have preserved the practices of an ancient fetishism, a poetry of noise and gesticulations which had its full meaning in forests haunted by monsters. Over the muffled pounding of the drums can be heard the clear laughter of copper castanets. At the head of the procession a few negroes dance – naturally, for the pleasure of it. These leaping dances speak of a pure black Africa. By contrast, the Moorish dance, or belly dance, in certain of its slow postures, carries a reminder of sacred dance from the more metaphysical East.

Behind the raucous and ape-like musicians, the crowd of slaves sing a half-Arab, half-Sudanese chant, interrupted by shrill, monotonous refrains.

A group of children buzz like a swarm of flies. The little negroes are unaffectedly comic, with their tufts of hair stuck on their little gleaming scalps, and their dirty shirts. The white children are miniature *marabouts* in brightly coloured *gandouras*, their skin slightly coppery from the sun. They look almost Chinese: fine-featured, and with their single plait of glossy hair trailing down their backs from the tops of their shaved heads. They all laugh at the noise and uproar, the gaudy display, and dance around the impassive Sudanese, who vaguely remember that their festival is a rite sacred to their race.

The musicians cease playing, kick off their sandals and come first to kiss the *marabouts'* clothing, then they form themselves in a semi-circle and resume their racket.

Two of the singers enter the semi-circle and, face to face, begin to dance, leaping like monkeys into the air and landing in a crouch. Their feet strike the earth and they clap the rosy palms of their hands above their heads. All their ancient negro blood stirs and overflows, triumphing over the artificial habit of reserve imposed by slavery. They become themselves again, both innocent and wild, eager for childlike games and barbarous frenzy, very near, now, to our animal origins.

One of the dancers in particular works himself up into madness, an old man with a sunken face, long yellow teeth, and ecstatic eyes.

For me, this spectacle of savagery has a harsh taste here in this simple setting, against the dull background of brick walls now turning pink in the sun.

The Sudanese suddenly fall prostrate to earth. After a second of stillness, a little death, they half raise themselves, laboriously crouching, and facing Sidi Brahim.

A strong odour of beast rises from their sweaty veils and

[77]

from their skin, which appears even blacker under its sheen of sweat.

Their hands come up before their faces, palms open, like books.

Sidi Brahim recites the 'Fatiha', the first chapter of the Koran. Then he implores the benediction of God and of Sidi M'Hammed Ben-Bou-Ziane upon the blacks, upon all present, the inhabitants of the territory of Kenadsa, upon all the Zianias and all Muslim men and women, dead or living.

Afterwards the *marabout* prays God to protect and aid, in all times and all places, the servant of the Lord and of his Prophet, Si Mahmoud ould Ali the Algerian.... I bow, deeply moved by his consideration.

As the Night Breathes

It is the hour of sunset, bringing refreshment with the first breath of night, when the brick walls give off all the heat they have accumulated during the day. So in the houses it's stifling as an oven, but outside it's fine and soothing in the first shadows. I stay a long time, lazily stretched out, my gaze steeped in the wave of lilac sky. And I listen to the last sounds fade in the *zawiya* and the *ksar*: doors that creak and close heavily, horses whinnying, goats bleating on the terraces, brayings of the small African donkeys – so sad, like sobbing – and the negresses' sharp voices.

Nearer, in the courtyard, there are sounds of tambourines and of fragile, two-stringed guitars accompanying strange vocal melodies, more like keening than like music. From time to time the voices plunge and fade, all is hushed, the blood alone speaks.

Life resumes and on the terraces of the houses slaves

appear, settling themselves on mats, rugs, or sacks.

The ear strains to hear stifled sounds of the kitchen, quarrels between lowered voices, murmured prayers. And the nostrils stir at the smells carried their way from a tangle of black bodies, lit by the hearth fires' joyful flames. Upon the doors of the *marabouts'* houses, other profiles are silhouetted. This is daily life, all the life of the *ksar*, and I take it in as something known for all time, and always new.

Towards the right, beyond the Mellah, a stretch of wall remains bright, even this late. Strange shadows play on its reddish surface. Sometimes they wave back and forth, slowly; sometimes they set up a hectic dance. After all the voices fall silent, when everything around is asleep, the Aissawas are still awake. In the imperceptibly freshening night these enlightened brethren strike the tambourine and blow strident laments on the *rhaita*. They sing, too, slowly, as in a dream.

Their sweaty bodies sway in an accelerating rhythm before the glowing braziers wafting their fumes of benzoin and myrrh. From the music, their swaying, and the intoxicating smoke, the Aissawas seek forgetfulness and sensual ecstasy.

There's something else I hear. I can make out other forms, now that even the Aissawas are dozing. A sound of panting comes to trouble me from over by the terraces. I suspect, I know, I listen: sighs and groanings in the cinnamon-scented night. Under the tranquil stars, the passionate rut. The languor of the warm night reawakens desire, mingles flesh with flesh in these embraces, another kind of fear: to feel the teeth clamp in a mortal spasm, the rattle in the lungs . . . What anguish! I'm on the verge of wrestling the warm earth itself – but true sensuousness is higher: in the stars' scintillation, in the memory of eyes one recognizes and of hours dwelt in, hours so beautifully lost.

A while ago the enlightened Aissawas were singing their Asiatic ballads, celebrating the blessedness of non-existence. And now the black Africans are singing, unthinkingly, a great hymn of love to eternal fecundity. As for me, I know music stranger and stronger, music that would bleed the heart into silence, songs that lips have murmured, absent lips that will drink other breath than mine, that will breathe another soul than mine, because my soul could not give itself, because it was not in me but in eternal things, and I possess it finally only in the vast, the divine solitude of all my being offered to the southern night.

In the morning, the west wind suddenly arrived. This wind, which could be seen coming, raised spirals of dust like tall plumes of dark smoke. It advanced on the calmness of the air, with great sighs that soon became howls; I lent it living accents, I felt myself carried up in the huge embrace of monstrous wings rushing to destroy everything. And the sand fell upon the terraces with the incessant small sound of a shower.

A Gathering of Students

Yesterday evening the slave Farradji came looking for me, very conspiratorially, to let me know that Si El Madani and a few other students at the mosque wished to invite me to tea.

I couldn't help recalling the descriptions of wild orgies which Moulieras's book, *The Unknown Morocco*, attributes to Moroccan students, and wondering why Farradji was taking such precautions in transmitting the invitation.

I've met El Madani, brother of Si Mohammed Laredj, many times at prayer. He's a small, thin young man, with polite manners. Anyway, I accept the invitation.

We cross the empty stables and silent courtyards, passing among the twisted trunks of hundred-year-old trees. No one in this quarter. Our steps echo on the paving stones.

At the end of a dark, damp maze of corridors piled with rocks and debris, we suddenly enter a delightful small courtyard surrounded by arches that once were white. Above the wall, the head of a date tree with its curved fronds can be seen nodding beyond on the terrace. A virgin vine climbs the length of a pillar and winds itself around the oblique trunk of the palm, then falls again in a cataract of leaves and tiny grapes.

Si El Madani and a group of students come to meet me, welcoming me with great courtesy. These are the sons of *marabouts* or of villagers: pale, frail, withered by living too long in the gloom of the *ksar*.

Si Abd el Djebbar, a Hamian nomad from Mecheria who has come to study at the *zawiya*, stands out from the rest. He is a head taller than the settlers, a son of frontier warriors: robust, muscular, holding himself with masculine pride, he has fine, well balanced features, bronze skin, and his long brown eyes shine with the flame of intelligence.

We enter the tearoom by a sculpted double door which creaks on rusty hinges. Within, a smoky twilight. The elegance of its fine columns, and the lacy frieze of arabesques cut in the milky stone combine to make it a very pleasant room. A few small dormer windows, opening from a cupola on to the bright watered-silk of the sky, spill a pale light on to the walls' green Egyptian faience tiles and patches of scabby plaster.

A stone step leads to the second, raised half of the vast apartment. There, some rugs from Rabat and mattresses of white wool carpet the floor.

Under the black beams of the ceiling, which are intertwined with red- and green-coloured reeds, a short inscription runs all around the walls, painted in vermilion letters: 'el afia el bakia' – eternal health.

In little niches, on shelves, on large coffers painted with flowers of dull gold, a jumble of objects is piled. Arabic books, cooking utensils, bits of clothing and harness, musical instruments and weapons, are thrown together in charming disarray. Amongst the ordinary pottery from Bechar, a graceful Venetian pitcher focuses the light in its crystal. Copper Aladdin's lamps, a green porcelain vase embellished with trefoils, faience with its molten colours – and, the ultimate visual treat: under a drape of brilliant silk, ranged around the platters and tea service, little multi-coloured glasses offer themselves like wildflowers.

I settle myself near the latticed window which looks out on a chaos of weathered ruins. These buildings, which once sheltered humans, now fall into dust and return to the baked earth from which they rose.

Farradji and his brother Khaddou light some dry palm branches in the courtyard while Si El Madani explains, without my asking him, the reason for the secrecy surrounding their invitation.

'You know, Si Mahmoud, custom and propriety demand that our parents and superiors not know of our pleasures, or may at least pretend not to know of them. We come here to pass a few hours, lifting our spirits with music, poetry, and good conversation. What happens here no one except God and ourselves should know about . . . otherwise, however innocent our diversions, we would be greatly shamed by them and severely reproached. That's why I have chosen this apartment, the only one still habitable in this old *kasbah* which my grandfather left me. No one comes near here – no one to advise us, or take control of our moments of freedom.'

The gathering passes in conversation. As if to emphasize the recreational privacy of it, one of the Muslim scholars, after the introductions were made, resumed his needlework, choosing silks for a white *gandoura* that he's decorating with fine embroidery. Among Moroccan students, needlework and ornamentation of fabric are highly honoured: such employments are a mark of taste and are in no way in decline; they are simply not practised in public.

El Madani takes a three-stringed guitar and begins nonchalantly to sing an old Andalusian motif which winds and curls around a single note. His cousin, Mouley Idris, a skinny adolescent with a peevish expression, accompanies him timidly on the tambourine. The handsome Hamiani, Abd el Djebbar, sees nothing in the music but a motive for yawning; lying full length on the carpet like a big Saluki hound, he stretches his lean horseman's muscles, which are clearly unused to inactivity.

I listen to the languorous, sad song, and day-dream about the lives of these Muslim students: the long tradition of scholastic studies within the bare, simple confines of the ancient mosques; pious exercises stirring most of these young men, already affiliated with mystical brotherhoods, to daily ecstasy.

But this austere regimen hides their simple gaiety, and a passionate sensuality which leads to the most complex and dangerous adventures, and – I must admit, especially here in the west – many hidden vices. An almost cloistered life promotes this perversion of the senses.

One fine day the Moroccan student, submitting without complaint to paternal authority, marries joylessly. Then his existence changes, dreams and studies banished from it. He enters society; he no longer lives in the realm of his personal vices, his feline sensuality. He takes on the manners of his people, calm and imposing, a face correct and unmoving. Quite often he will come to regret the voluptuous atmosphere of the carefree 'bith-es-sohfa', the gathering place, the students' common den.

Whether *marabout* or leading citizen, the young scholar quickly assumes an air of importance. A few years, even months suffice to change his character deeply. He takes part in the deliberations of the *djemaa*, and a legislator does not do too much thinking for himself. He goes to war, or travels

[83]

the Muslim world, perhaps making the pilgrimage to Mecca.

Ancestral obligations rescind all his rights and leave hardly anything to the individual for his self-development. He quickly becomes the man of his milieu, and takes pleasure and pride in being so. When after some years these former students, singers, and verse readers have seen their sons grow up, they will pitilessly impose the same severe rule under which they chafed as young men, and the new generation will be led in its turn to secret pleasures.

For the well-born Muslim at home, particularly in towns, nothing of personal affairs, family life, pleasures, or loves, must be revealed outside. The publicizing of pleasures, as European students love to do, is unknown in the Islamic world. From their earliest years, Moroccan scholars are bound to hide their joy. This explains their fiery yet controlled nature, their strong, interior passions so seldom allowed to surface, their all-embracing intellectuality that, still, so quickly fades.

The hour passes. My ideas turn nebulous. I give myself up to the melancholy and antique charm of the instruments, content to be still, here where resignation is constant and unchanging, where everything faces death without a shudder, serenely, under the setting sun of Islam. The red letters of the motto encircling the walls extend their arabesques into the darkness. My mind grows calm under an ivory caress.

. . . The contact of time possessed is like that of a cold, pale hand on a burning forehead. . . .

The strength and quietude of things that seem to go on forever, because they proceed gently towards emptiness; without fuss, revolt or agitation, without even a tremble – towards inevitable death.

* * *

Evening – one more evening – falls upon the sleepy *zawiya*. Long lines of veiled women aflame with bright colours make their way to the fountain as others have for two centuries, with the same strong, supple gait, bare feet solidly placed on the powdery earth – those others who passed this way and are now no more than a handful of dust scattered among the small stones in Lella Aicha's cemetery.

The light wind trembles in the stiff fronds of an enormous, heroic date palm rising behind the wall like a thicket of spears. Of all trees, the date most resembles the column of a temple. There is something of war and of mysticism, belief in the One, and aspiration in this branchless tree. Islam, like the date palm, embodies justice and a bursting forth into the light. Islam is the divine expression of palms and sprays of water.

An infinite calm descends into the turmoil of my weary soul. My lightness comes from myself, from the weight of a sweltering day finally lifted, and from the relief of lengthening shadows on my dry eyelids.

It is the welcome hour when, in the highland towns, alcoholic consolations are poured on lazy brains. When the sky sings over the towns, man feels the need to sing in unison with it, and, lacking any inspiration, he drinks out of his need for an ideal and for enthusiasm.

Happy is he who can get drunk on his own thought, and who knows how to etherize by the heat of his soul the very spokes of the universal wheel!

For a long time I was incapable. I suffered from my weakness and my indifference. Now, far from the crowds and carrying in my heart unforgettable words of strength, no drunkenness is equal to that which a golden-green sky opens up in me. Led by a mysterious force, I have found here what I was seeking, and I taste a blessed repose in conditions where others would shudder with boredom.

One day, a frail young woman who was watching her too pale blood evaporate under the Algerian sky, lay languid on the cushions of her *chaise longue*, listening to the noisy gangs descending from the heights of Mustapha one Sunday evening. She said to me, 'Life must be sad that they should sing about it so loudly!'

But then, we have all more or less made some noise. It was our student wildness exerting itself.

The sufferings of love must have ennobled our destiny. We avoided casting our anchor into the shallows of happiness where our existence would have passed, balanced on the tame little waves of daily life. We can applaud ourselves for having known the earth and having recognized the place, however small, that could be occupied by the largest thought. Here we have touched a corner of the world where no one is tainted by the thirst for innovations. The material life, however, leaves its mark deeply imprinted.

So what are the events which impassion these nomads, representatives of the most ancient past, and these serene *marabouts* who, disdaining labour, bathe their brows in a covenantal light? Their life passes before my eyes for me to reflect upon.

I wish again this evening to see my reflection in this precious water of the south. I wish again to drink the water sought by the women at the desert fountain, to feel it flow over my feverish hands, to see it drip from my fingers like beads of highest wisdom. . . .

The Return of the Flock

Beside me on the radiant terrace Ba Mahmadou ou Salem is softly singing the old litanies of the Prophet. In the red western light his dark face has a bronze patina and his white veils glow.

Suddenly into the somnolent silence of the *ksar* a clamour of voices intrudes, followed by doors creaking, confused brayings and joyful cries: 'Here's the *harrag* returned! They're leading back the *harrag*!' And indeed, we see the unhoped-for return of the *marabouts*' and villagers' large flock, stolen recently by Arab pillagers and Berbers of the Ait Khebbach tribe.

The robbers had driven the flock westward, but the local Ziani *sherif*, Mouley Ahmed, finding out where the booty came from, told his people that they had committed a great sin by stealing the *zawiya*'s flock from holy territory. 'You have deprived the poor, travellers, and orphans,' he explained to them. 'If you want God and Sidi Brahim Ben-Bou-Ziane to grant you their blessings, you will return these animals without delay.'

After some hesitation, the bandits gave in to Mouley Ahmed's injunctions and designated one of their allies, El Hassani of the Ait Atta Berbers, to bring back the *harrag* to Kenadsa and to beg pardon of Sidi Brahim on their behalf.

The slaves run to announce the good news to the *marabout*, just finishing his prayers in the cool darkness of his large white apartments. Not wanting to miss the pardoning scene, I follow the *marabout* down.

Black goats invade the courtyard, crowding each other and leaping, panicked, taking refuge even in the horses' long manger. Three men on foot drive them, black slaves from Bou Dnib who are heavily armed.

The Berber El Hassani, mounted on a thin grey horse, dismounts before the great door.

Sidi Brahim, his hand resting on the shoulder of little Messaoud, comes forward slowly, with difficulty, through the confusion of the flock. 'Be welcome, my sons! God reward you for your good work!'

Then these hard men piously kiss the *marabout*'s veils and

hands; he, quite moved, embraces them in turn, in a scene of immemorial forgiveness.

People of the West

El Hassani is a young man of middle height, beardless, lean, and muscular. He wears modest clothing of very clean white wool. On his head is wound the *tercha*, a little round turban. Leather straps, passing between his toes, attach his nomad's sandals to his feet. There is energy and intelligence in his pale, thin face, and a mocking smile strays often over his fine lips. El Hassani has gunpowder in his veins.

While the negroes of Bou Dnib exchange greetings and embraces with their brothers of Kenadsa, the Berber remains seated near the wall, his Winchester carbine between his knees. He waits, indifferent and silent.

Sidi Brahim comes to ask me, when we have reascended the terrace, whether I would mind if El Hassani and Mouley Sahel (one of the Bou Dnib blacks) lodged with me. I accept this arrangement with curiosity. Then for a long while the *marabout* talks to me about the Berbers.

'If ever you wish to travel further west, the Berbers and above all the Ait Atta will be your best guides. When one of them says to you, "You are under God's finger and mine; I am accountable for your safety", you may confidently go anywhere he leads you. You'll return safe and sound, unless you both die together. The Berbers never betray their sworn oath.'

Then the *marabout* added, laughing: 'For the moment, you'll see how clever they can be if you keep your eye on El Hassani there in the courtyard.'

From the height of the terrace I glance down over the

[88]

battlements into the courtyard, crowded with slaves and villagers milling about, identifying the goats. El Hassani, indifferent to all the tumult, is still at his post, satisfied that he has fulfilled his mission.

Sidi Brahim then leans over and calls to the Berber: 'Come join us, my son, up here on the terrace.'

The Berber rises and smiles. He hefts his rifle on to his shoulder and bundles his burnous into a packet which, with one vigorous, efficient motion, he throws at our feet. For an instant he inspects the smooth brick wall which is six or seven metres high. Then with a monkey's agility, he jumps and clings by his fingernails and bare feet to rough places I can't even make out. Almost in a single bound, he is on the parapet of the terrace. What a climber!

'Si El Hassani,' I tell him, 'it is certainly preferable to be your friend than your enemy, for where could one flee from you? Walls don't exist for you.'

He smiles and answers with perfect good grace: 'Mouley Mahmoud, all those who serve Sidi M'Hammed Ben-Bou-Ziane are my brothers and my friends.' He speaks Arabic with a slight accent which is, however, not that of other Berbers. El Hassani has the calm and easy manners of a man who knows his own worth, who feels sure of himself. Mouley Sahel, his black companion who is content to climb by the stairs, speaks to him in the Berber language, laughingly urging him on to something. Giving in to the request of his companion, rather than out of boastfulness, El Hassani tells us about an adventure he had three years ago.

'I and my brothers, the Ait Atta, wished to take vengeance on the people of a *ksar* situated on the road to Tafilala. There was a chase. As night was approaching, we decided to occupy a little *kasbah*, which was isolated and well sealed. I climbed the wall in order to open the doors. At the top, as I was about to descend into the interior, I was ambushed by four or five of our enemies hidden in the courtyard. They attacked me with gunshots and stones. I intended to stay on the top of the wall in order to shoot easily at these dogs, but my clothing — actually my underclothing — caught on the point of a beam and knocked me off balance. So, hanging in mid-air, but with my arms free, I began to fire. I know I killed two of them, those who had rifles; as for the others, they took off and jumped the opposite wall thinking to flee into the country-side, but my companions brought them down in the *alfa*. Inside the *kasbah* there was some ground wheat, some goat-skins of butter, a fresh cistern and sweet dates: we had a good meal in return for our trouble.'

El Hassani recounts this story as a minor, droll incident in his life as a scaler of walls. Then Sidi Brahim takes his leave.

The two men from the west, tired, lie down on the rug, their rifles under their folded burnous which serve as pillows. They fall asleep quickly. I alone remain awake in the pale light of the moon.

These travellers will leave again tomorrow. They will pass like fantastic shades through my life, gesturing like panto-mime warriors. I dream about other, less handsome Panta-loons, moved by less solid stage-tricks. I imagine El Hassani firing into the void, encircled by an audience of Europeans applauding him from their crimson velvet banquettes, as they munch on sweets. I dream, too, about what Sidi Brahim was telling me: how easy it would be to leave one day with men like these, to set off with my dream and my thirst for the unknown through all the *zawiyas* of Morocco, to Bou Dnib, to Tafilala, towards the far-off Tisnit, all the way down to the entrance of the great empty desert.

* * *

Encounter at Night

I was returning by the Bou Dnib road from a ride on horse-back to the salt plains, with Maamar ould Kaddour and a few Rzaina nomads, *mokhazni* from Bechar who were on a pilgrimage to Kenadsa. Under the oppressive heat of the moon-lit night a torpid sensuality filled the sleepy gardens. Rustlings like contented, subdued sighs mounted into the stillness. Life was welling up, inexhaustible, through all the pores of the earth and of the overburdened plants.

Tired, we had approached in silence, and our horses walked noiselessly over the fine sand. In a narrow alley, between two clay walls, they stopped to drink from a clear *seguia*.

Suddenly Maamar touched me on the shoulder. Under the palm trees in the garden were a nomad and a woman from the *ksar*, standing close to one another.

I recognized the Arab by his high Algerian turban. It was Abd el Djebbar, the Hamiani, whom I met at the Kenadsa mosque, among the students. He was murmuring, 'I am your brother . . . for the love of God, be mine!' And his strong hands grasped the frail wrists of the young, waxen-faced village girl.

She was lovely, and adorned like a bride. A long tunic of red wool draped her curves. Her forehead was wreathed with silver flowers, and the moonlight was mirrored in the lustre of her jewellery. The stars seemed to weep for the smoothness of her brow.

She had come to this rendezvous recklessly, in the night so calm yet full of snares. And now she was trembling, was begging mercy of the handsome nomad, descended from a different race, whose savage ardour frightened her.

It seemed to me that Abd el Djebbar's heart beat so strongly that I could hear it behind the wall. His arms entwined the girl and lifted her off the ground in an embrace. She resisted, about to cry out. But the nomad's eager mouth arrested her cry of distress, his kiss stifling it, biting it off abruptly.

Then the two bodies, convulsing in love's superb fury, rolled together upon the shadowy earth that's as welcoming of fecundity as of death.

At this moment Maamar spurred his horse, making it prance, and with a strangled laugh said, 'Leave them! We sons of Arabs know how to love. We gamble our lives for women but when we take them in the night, like the hunter of gazelles, we press them against us in a way they'll remember. Afterward, no *ksourian* can make them forget the nomad's kiss.'

Their shadows, embracing, then merged with the garden's verdure. We went our way, leaving behind this vision of love and daring.

The Oblivion Seekers

I have discovered a *kif* house in the *ksar* – where there isn't even a café, and people have no other place to gather than the public square and the earthen benches at the foot of the ramparts. It's in a sort of half-ruined house behind the Mellah, a long room lit by a single skylight set among the ceiling's smoky, twisted beams. The walls are black, furrowed with lighter cracks like wounds. On the tamped earth floor, somewhat powdery and rarely swept, are scattered pomegranate skins and other trash.

This strange place serves as a refuge for Moroccan vagabonds, nomads, and all kinds of homeless, sickly-looking people. The house seems to belong to no one; a suspicious kind of inn, where one is ill advised to spend a night. It has the look of a stage set for some theatrical crime plot.

In one corner there's a clean mat, with some leather cushions from Fez. On the mat stands a large Arab chest, brightly painted, which serves as a table. Nearby is a bush with small, pale-pink flowers overhanging an herbal bouquet. The herbs soak in a fat, highland jar decorated with geometric designs and arabesques. Further away, a copper kettle on a tripod, two or three teapots, and a basket stuffed with dried Indian hemp. That is the entire décor, the whole setting for the little *kif*-smokers'club made up of people who are fond of their comforts.

I almost forgot: on a makeshift perch of palm stalks, a captive vulture hulks, attached by the foot.

The strangers and wanderers who haunt this lair sometimes join up with the *kif* smokers, even though the latter make up a very closed little association, very difficult to enter. Travellers themselves, who cross the Muslim world in their reverie, the hallucinogenic devotees who gather at Kenadsa belong to an even more exclusive class than the scholars.

Hadj Idris is a tall, thin Filali, with a tanned, good-natured face that seems illumined from within. He is one of those rootless men without family or profession, so numerous in the Muslim world. For twenty-five years he has travelled from town to town, working or begging as the occasion warrants. He plays the *goumbri*, a small Arab guitar with two strings stretched on a tortoise shell, and a neck of sculpted wood. His beautiful, deep voice is well suited for singing the old Andalusian ballads, with their melancholy, tender airs.

Si Mohammed Behaouri, a Moroccan from Meknes, has a pale complexion and endearing eyes. Still young, he is a poet, wandering across Morocco and southern Algeria in quest of legends and Arabic folk-tales; for his living, he composes and recites verses about the delights and agonies of love.

Another comes from Djebel Zerhaoun. Physician and sorcerer, small, spare, muscular, tanned by the Sudanese sun, he roamed with the caravans from the Senegalese coast to Timbuktu. Over the course of his days, he will go on slowly measuring out medicines and leafing through old books of spells from the Mogh'rib.

[93]

Chance has reunited these people in Kenadsa. Tomorrow they will be off, scattered upon their various roads, all going unconcernedly towards the accomplishment of their destinies. The community of their tastes has reassembled them in this smoky refuge, where they glide over the slow hours of their lives, free from care.

In the evening an oblique, rosy beam from the skylight slices the room's penumbra. The *kif* smokers huddle together, their turbans adorned with pungent sprigs of basil. They range themselves along the wall, reclining on their mat, and smoke their little red clay pipes filled with hemp and crumbled Moorish tobacco.

Hadj Idris stuffs the pipes and passes them around, after carefully wiping the stem against his cheek, out of politeness. When his pipe is empty, he delicately gathers the little ember remaining at the bottom and pops it in his mouth – he doesn't feel it burn – then, the pipe refilled, he uses this cinder to relight the little fire which, over the coming hours, will smoulder continuously. Extremely intelligent, with a fine and penetrating mind, yet easy-going in his constant half-drunkenness, he nurses his dream with the stupefying smoke.

The oblivion seekers sing while lazily clapping their hands; their dreamy voices rise late into the night, by the dim flame of a lantern with mica panes. Then little by little the voices grow fainter, slower, more breathless; finally the smokers are silenced, their gaze fixed upon their flowers, in ecstasy.

These are epicureans, sensualists, perhaps sages who, in this black den, among Moroccan vagabonds, can distinguish charms on every horizon, can build marvellous cities where contentment abides.

* * *

After the prayer of *asr*, around four o'clock, the sun begins to descend over the rocky hills of Morocco. The overheated earth exhales its weariness of the ruthless day; yet the evil hours of torpor and prostration have passed. I'm flushed with a sense of well-being, as when I've narrowly escaped some danger, or woken to deliverance from a nightmare; and accompanied by a slave I venture slowly into the gardens, scaling the low walls that divide them.

At Kenadsa there are no large palm groves as at Figuig or Bechar: the gardens are coaxed out of the open desert, to struggle weakly against the sand's slow but determined invasion from the deadly dryness of the neighbouring *hamada*. These gardens consist of families of date trees, five or six sprung from the same stump; fruit trees, casting sparser shadows, whose velvety fruits fall into the *seguias*; and the parsimonious water supply that carries refreshment to the compact, golden fields which have yielded the meagre barley harvest.

Against the walls, in the tangle of vines and lianas entwining the palm and pomegranate trees, and under the broad, burgeoning fig trees, there are corners of shade, deliciously cool.

Here and there, wide green ponds receive the overflow from the irrigation streams, and countless little toads purl their melancholy song along their banks.

The gardens are cultivated by farmers, most of them black, in exchange for a fifth of the crop. They live there during the slow days' work among the trees, helping each other to embellish the charming disorder of their plantations. All of them grow *zafour*, with its rich, orange flowers used by the women for dyeing fabric and for make-up. Some of the farmers know how to support the frail plants with the branches of a wild bush which grows long, thin clusters of mauve flowers; others plant clumps of violet asters, taken from the desert wadis. I feast my eyes on the tall rose bushes with hundreds of leaves, called Syrian roses.

The farmers, ever hospitable, hasten to provide us with tea. Slung in the panels of their soiled burnous they bring small, golden apricots and almonds: the *zawiya*'s guest is welcome among them.

One evening the eldest of them, an old Moroccan of the Sedjaa tribe, all bent over, with a mummified face, brought me a bunch of pomegranates and a plait of onions.

'You see, the flowers and fruits of my garden are not plentiful; I'm a poor old man and have nothing else to offer you in welcome. Accept these few vegetables. God is the bestower of all wealth! Accept my humble offering and pardon me.'

I didn't dare refuse this simple and touching present, for fear of offending the old gardener who looked at me so bashfully, as if he were beholden to me for the produce of his garden.

At the edges of the *seguias*, mints and basil grow in the shade; pale, emaciated, yet piercingly fragrant; their perfume hovers in the evening air, with other vegetal scents more tenuous, undefinable.

In these Kenadsa gardens I rediscover the calm and the sweet sleepiness of other Saharan gardens, but without the mysterious, oppressive 'something' which seems to lie at the heart of vast palm groves and forests.

The day retreats. The date trees are soaked in sunset. We leave the gardens where the temperature will start to climb. Broad violet shadows stretch out from the rocks that redden in the sun's last rays.

Eternal drunkenness of southern evenings, quotidian and never the same – for as long as I live I will never tire of feeling your energy flow through me! This sad hour: its beauty and isolation and almost agonizing hold on me; the moment the desert suddenly darkens and contracts, as if to guard forever against intruders wishing to cross its desolate threshold, to delve into its delights!

Love at the Well

Along the pathway that borders the ramparts, the women from the *ksar* come to the well of Sidi Embarek. Under the oblique rays of the dying sun their veils become drenched in extraordinary hues. The fabrics shimmer, glorified, resembling precious brocades. From a distance you'd take them to be dressed in the rarest silks, embroidered with gold and gems. Aware of their attractions, the women move self-consciously, flitting from group to group, and the startling gamut of colours shifts unceasingly, like a mobile rainbow.

Some of them, the Sudanese or especially the nomads, are conspicuous for their graceful movements, faultless posture, the roundness of their hips, and the curve of an arm as it raises a full vessel to a shoulder.

There are others whose faces, though handsome, deviate from conventional prettiness and coquettishness because of an expression of sensuality, both timid and wild at the same time. In the midst of this unfeigned hypocrisy, which may be only an assertion of modesty, there passes suddenly, as through a mask, the flash of an unexpected smile, an unchecked burst of warmth.

A strong odour of moist skin and cinnamon wafts through the warm air from the clusters of women.

Some men, negroes and nomads, tribesmen of the Doui Menia, Ouled Djerir, and Ouled Nasser, come to water their horses. While the black slaves laugh and joke openly with the women, the desert men eye them discreetly, their pupils bright with desire.

How many intrigues are concocted here, beside the Sidi Embarek well, while the tired horses stretch their noses towards the fresh water of the spring?

By means of subtle gestures and brief glances, nomads and village women come to an understanding and commit themselves to a propitious time and place later that night.

Once again I glimpse some of the poetry of Arab loves, of nomad loves, which so often end in bloodshed.

The Jewesses, less protected, more audacious, freely accost the men, scattering provocative leers from under their eyelids which are reddened by the bitter palm smoke of the Mellah's dark stalls.

This is a time of freedom and gaiety when, removed from the iron control of their men, the women chatter and laugh, and play the dangerous game.

Faced with this primitive ritual, I recall other romances, trivial and complicated, basically the same as these – unless the essence of love is just in its varied courtship, and in its endurance of the impossible, rather than in the rash act. . . . But for how many beings is this true?

Under other colours, not so beautiful as these simple veils, where the body is still visible, passion prowls the towns, so often ugly, even repugnant – a hungry passion demanding life, desiring to perpetuate life, over and over again. Higher, further, disguised by intelligence and studied smiles, in the most correct salons, or like here near a desert fountain, the violence of this appetite betrays itself again, enflaming the eyes, altering the voice, draining the colour from trembling lips.

Oh how I have lived already in all men and in all women! And how many times was I saddened by this eternal sensuality coursing through the world's veins, revealing to me the dreadful image of the Fates.

Now I can follow this natural pastime painlessly, even with amusement. Love here has no other end but itself, and

[98]

perhaps we should try to restore it to this, in order to humiliate ourselves before nature, to blaspheme what has no function in us, that useless organ, this unquiet soul, which will never find any rest.

Desert Gypsies

I love seeing examples of the various indigenous races, so diverse yet still able to remain fairly pure. Here, for example, are some strange women, strange even to these parts, approaching from a camp of Doui Menia Ouled Slimane, who have stopped for a few days at the foot of the Barga, east of Lella Aicha's tomb.

The Menia women are taller and skinnier than women from the *ksar*, but sturdier, too, under their dark blue veils. Their puzzling elegance consists in what you might call 'the art of wearing rags'.

That a woman with jewellery, tinsel, ribbons, dressed hair, stylish clothes, affectations, pungent perfumes, all the dressmaker's skill, can look like a scarecrow, is borne out by most Jewesses in Algiers who have renounced their traditional costume to dress as French women. By contrast, the wives of pillaging nomads, draped in their tattered wool, have a quickness of gait which is almost athletic. They are perhaps the only women in Africa who know how to walk with pride. The poor cloth that veils their nudity seems to be of a piece with their bronzed architecture. When the lashing wind reduces them, plastering their tunics against their muscular legs, their outlines against the coppery skies and the paleness of deadened earth are like those of lanky she-wolves. You'd say they were as old as time, convinced that they no less than the males bring back to the lair their full share of booty.

[99]

Despite intermarriages with Berbers, which have watered down the tendency toward raw-boned faces and olive skin, there remains a certain Semitic expression which hearkens back to an untamed, Asian ancestry. Semiramis's warriors must have had these gaunt contours and the same eyes, long and tawny, like those of the black Saluki hounds.

These women have gestures I've never seen among Arab women, still less among the Moorish: they walk without timidity and without wavering before the men of other tribes. They seem to lack any coquettishness, and their lips form open, spontaneous smiles compared to those of the sensuous Sudanese and the complaisant Jewesses.

A man from the south regards the Jewess as impure. Nomads are never drawn to the white, rather anaemic beauty of the Mellah women. The two races skirt one another tolerantly without ever mixing. At times the Jew is necessary to shepherd and marauder alike, sometimes occasioning bitter arguments; but once a bargain is struck no other interest, no other thought brings them together.

These Doui Menia women are, though you'd least expect it, the gypsies of the desert. Their wild beauty, glimpsed through the holes in their tunics, is the colour of earth. Poverty for them is a natural thing, not a disgrace. They figure that all luxury resides in a horse's beauty, or in a dagger's haft.

In the Mellah

After nightfall, the cacophony down by the fountain quietens little by little within the larger, gaping silence of the valley.

I know all the songs of the African darkness and their dryness in the throat, but tonight I will not be lulled by my memories. Oh for a little of the hum and buzz of ordinary things, for places where life rumbles happily and gets on about its business without worry. To be simply animal, ignorant of forbidden gardens and terraces of deathly silence; to be loquacious and to shine, mindless, projecting brief and leaping shadows on to the screen of deep, indifferent night.

How I suffer from all the books I have read, from all the voices that have spoken to me, from all the paths I haven't taken! My soul's emptiness is made of a huge sigh. . . . I want a place of singing, of shouting, where I can forget myself for an hour, a public place ringing with arguments, a dark café where smoke curls past the windows – there I'll be a little sailor who gets drunk on homesickness, and a three-note song.

Everything is so clear here, too clear! No more obstacles to overcome, no more progress, no more action. You wouldn't know how to act anymore, or almost how to think: you'd die of eternity. . . .

Here's the gate in the ramparts. Pass through. Beyond, in the Mellah, it's like a great magic lantern. It's like going to a show, to see shapes dancing in the fire.

In front of their doors, the Jewesses have improvised hearth fires on which to cook the evening meal in big witches' cauldrons. There's nothing more picturesque than this kind of illumination.

The long flames from the dry palm fronds, and the dim glow of burning camel dung, cast upward on to the white-washed façades and brick walls a fleeting patina of red-gold and hot pink.

In the flickering light of this multitude of fires, bizarre apparitions loom, reflections climb the fronts of houses and run along the sand.

The men, crouching, apply themselves to small tasks by the light of smoky candle ends. They wait indefinitely with their shopkeepers' patience, so different from Arab attitudes.

The southern Jew's main difference from the Arab is his

vulgarity. He hasn't the least notion of what we call a noble sentiment; and in this lack resides, no doubt, the key to his insinuating and commercial abilities: he can adapt himself freely, unhindered by a character of his own.

A sudden blaze lights up the groups, heaped like bedded cattle, dark against the sand's rosy pallor. They give the impression of easy well-being. I am so familiar with their soul: it floats upon the steam from the cooking pots. I envy them. They are the critique of my romanticism, and of this incurable malaise I've brought from the north and from the mystic Orient, inherited from those who wandered before me in the steppe.

So when will I have done with this mania that leads me to interpret the simplest gestures in a religious sense? There is our Aryan weakness. When others cook their dinner, we think of the sacrifice of the Soma, of libations of butter on the fire. Just now a woman lifted a pot to add an armful of thorny wood to the fire: all that mattered to me was the flame shooting up, straight and free, towards the peacefulness of the stars.

Leaning against a section of broken-down wall, I continue to watch the tableaux of my magic lantern. Other images glide and shimmer in lively colours:

Children are playing, running back and forth between the light and dark, as wriggly as worms. Now and then a beautiful Jewess stands and stretches, tired, catlike in the sanguine glory of the flames bathing her in pink light, and tinting her paleness with an artificial flush. Her wide violet eyes with their heavy lids seem deeper then, more bruised, more earthy.

At length these visions of tranquil domesticity work their charm on me: Kenadsa's Mellah, ugly by day with poverty and hopeless filth, appears beautiful in this first hour of night; like a corner of some enchanted city, worshipper of potent and devouring fire.

Where, then, have I lived that I can recognize these things so profoundly?

A Jewess sings in a shrill voice, trying to calm her child's bitter cries. A donkey's melancholy braying is heard from a nearby stable. It is late; the women go inside. The fires burn down outside their closed doors.

In the distance, the *mueddins* cry out their call to prayer from an unfathomable sadness, and the numbing peace of Islam manages to erase the last trace of the transfigured Mellah.

That evening I slept soundly. This was one of my last nights of tranquillity and health. A short while after, fever ran me to ground and plunged me into strange dreams.

Recollections of Fever

Thin, supple-bodied negresses were dancing, bathed in blue light. In their midnight faces the enamel of their teeth gleamed through weird smiles. Their slender forms were draped in long veils of red, blue, or sulphur yellow which furled and unfurled in rhythm to their bizarre dance, floating on the wind and becoming at times as diaphanous as a cloud.

Their dark hands played the double iron castanets from the Sudanese festival. Sometimes the castanets would beat a savage rhythm, at others they clashed almost noiselessly.

But gradually the women became detached from the earth and floated into the air. Their bodies elongated, writhed, grew deformed, and whirled like the desert dust during an evening of sirocco winds. Finally they faded into the shadows among the smoky beams overhead.

My eyes opened weakly, lingering on the things around

[103]

me, seeking the strange creatures who, only moments before, were dancing for me.

I had seen them, I had heard their throaty laughter like muted cluckings; I had felt on my burning forehead the warm gusts that lifted their veils. They had disappeared, leaving me with an inexplicable longing. Where were they now?

My exhausted mind struggled to escape the limbo where it had drifted – for hours or centuries? I was no longer sure. It seemed to return from a black abyss where beings lived and things moved according to different laws than the ones that govern the world of reality, and my overheated brain strove painfully to chase away these haunting phantoms.

The Watery Paradise

A great silence was weighing on the slumbering *zawiya*. It was the deadly noon hour, the hour of mirage and of agonizing fever. Heat expanded over the glowing terraces and the scintillating dunes in the distance.

I had been put to bed in a nook that gave on to a high terrace. The little room opened to its full height on to the bleached sky and the rock and sand of the desert's inferno.

From the palmwood beams of the ceiling was hanging a small goatskin bottle, from which water was slowly dripping into a large copper plate set on the floor.

Every minute the drop fell, pinging on the metal clearly, regularly, with the monotony of a hospital or prison clock's tick-tock, and this noise was as excruciating as if the obstinate drop were falling on my flaming skull.

Squatting near me, Ba Mahmadou silently waved a fly-chaser made of long horsehairs, dyed with henna like the tail of a parade horse. I watched him. During moments as long as years I imagined the relief I would experience when he would lift the plate at my request, and the drop of water would finally be muffled on the beaten earth of the floor. But I was unable to speak, and the drop kept falling, clanging inexorably on the polished copper.

The beams of the ceiling vanished, becoming sky and silvery-blue palm fronds swinging and rustling overhead.

Around the tapering trunks of date palms, under their arched foliage, intensely green vines entwined themselves, and flowering pomegranates bled in the shade.

I was lying in a *seguia*, on long water-grasses, soft and enveloping as tresses of hair. Fresh water flowed over my body and I wallowed in its wet caress.

Another rivulet splashed within reach of my mouth. Sometimes, without moving, I received the icy water between my lips; I felt it go down my parched gullet into my chest where, gradually, the intolerable, burning thirst was extinguished. Water, salubrious water, blessed water of my delicious dreams!

I abandoned myself to numerous visions, to slow ecstasies of a watery paradise ... of immense green ponds under the graceful date palms; innumerable clear streams; swift cascades gurgling over mossy rocks; and all around the sound of wells creaking, distributing the treasures of life and fertility.

Somewhere far off a voice rose, a voice that shrieked in the silence without effect. It came from an unknown source, across vast spaces of verdure and shade.

The voice troubled my rest. Again my eyes opened on my little room of voluntary exile. The voice asserted itself as real, rose again: the man of the mosques was announcing the midday prayer.

Ba Mahmadou then raised the black forefinger of his right

hand; he attested to God's unity and Mohammed as his prophet; then he rose, gathering his white veils about his tall, ebony body.

He prayed. At each prostration his *koumia* knocked against the ground. He said, 'God is great', and bent over, his brow in the dust, facing Mecca. My eyes followed the slave's slow gestures.

When he finished his prayers, Ba Mahmadou returned to his place near me and resumed waving his long hennaed flychaser.

A red-brown shimmering went up from the terraces, which seemed about to split open. In the still air, heavy as molten metal, no breeze passed, not a breath. My clothes were soaked with sweat and there was a crushing weight on my chest. A burning thirst, an atrocious thirst that nothing could assuage, devoured me. My limbs were sore and tender, and my heavy skull rolled on the sack that was my pillow.

Ba Mahmadou soaked a scrap of muslin in water and moistened my face and chest. Then he poured a few drops of lukewarm mint tea into my mouth.

I sighed and stretched my swollen arms.

The *mueddin*'s voice died out over the *ksar*. My mind hovered again in vague regions peopled with strange apparitions, where blessed waters flowed.

The day of fire was extinguished in the rosy glow of the valley and hills. Beyond the *sebkhas*, the date palms were lit up like tall black candles.

Again the *mueddin* cried out his melancholy call. I was wakeful now. My eyes with their bruised and heavy lids opened avidly on the evening's splendour. Suddenly I was sunk in sadness, invaded by childish regrets.

I was alone, alone in this lost corner of Morocco, alone everywhere I had lived and alone wherever I should go, always. I had no country, no home, no family, and possibly no more friends. I had passed through, a stranger and intruder, arousing nothing but disapproval and dislike in those around me.

At that moment how I suffered: far from all comfort, among men who, unruffled, look on at the ruin of everything around them, and who cross their arms before sickness and death, saying '*mektoub*' – it is written.

Those who elsewhere on earth might have spared a thought for me were no doubt preoccupied by their own happiness. They weren't suffering in sympathy. Oh, *mektoub*, indeed!

More lucid, calmed, I scorned my weakness and smiled at my unhappiness. If I was alone, was it not what I desired? – desired consciously, my thoughts transcending cowardly sentimentalities of the heart and of my equally infirm flesh.

To be alone is to be free, and freedom has been the sole happiness required by my restless, impatient nature – an arrogant nature, none the less.

Then, I told myself that my solitude was a good thing. I desired it for myself, for my friends, for all those like myself. I desired it as our good, as the divine abode of our immortality.

I glimpsed an image of shining salons where others were dancing, smiling at idiocies, of theatre stalls where they were jostling each other; and I pitied them so. I crumpled between my withered hands the impoverished stuff of their dreams. I imagined the place of their graves, and then my own. . . . A great peace, melancholy and sweet, filled me. The hour passed.

A hot wind rose from the west, bringing more fever and anguish. My head, already tired, fell back on the pillow; my body was annihilated in almost voluptuous torpor; my limbs grew light, as if dissolving.

Summer night, dark and starry, fell over the desert. My mind left my body and flew again towards the enchanted gardens and the bluish reservoirs of the Watery Paradise.

Vivid Images

In my state of contented lassitude I haven't the strength for concentrated thought. Mental images come together only fleetingly. Ghostly scumbles and watercolour sketches, diaphanous and vague, will suddenly acquire the sharp contours of an etching, of scenes I had all but forgotten.

For a whole hour I saw myself again at Ain Sefra, having come across some notes I'd made there. As I leafed through them, they led me into the sort of childish images that play themselves out upon a sick bed.

At a Moorish café, among the colourful, wild crowd, there was a bewildered little rifleman. I see him very distinctly. He must be rather drunk. There he goes, starting to sing. Soon his high voice dominates all the others. He stops suddenly, letting his forehead fall on the next fellow's chest. The little skirmisher is weeping.

'Abdelkader,' he says, 'you see those caged turtle-doves? Well, they've made me cry, because they remind me of my father's house, at Frenda. We used to have pet turtle-doves, too. But I'll never see them again. My mother and father are dead, and the turtle-doves must be dead, too. . . .'

The scene changes:

In a deserted street which opens on to the low dunes of Tiout, bands of skirmishers are setting out in the hot sirocco winds. Month after month of hard nights on lonely bedrolls have made their rough hands shrivelled. Now the terrible stress of unappeased lust has propelled them into the two blind alleys of Djenan ed Dar, on a desperate search for a woman to hold on to.

Many of them have fallen into sorry affairs, in barracks, prisons, and penal camps. Now they are off to satisfy the tyrannical instinct of life demanding to perpetuate itself – off towards a sad hovel, lashed by the desert wind.

Eight o'clock. The riflemen who couldn't enter for lack of space within are stationed in front of the brothel. They yell and thump with fists and feet at the door, cracking it with their combined force.

Finally, a noise of heavy boots reverberates inside.

A savage, joyful clamour goes up from the group. Among them is my little soldier, the same who that afternoon was weeping over caged turtle-doves.

Amid bursts of laughter, he is already unbuckling his sword-belt.

Symphony of Words

I am taken again by fever. In order to focus my wandering ideas, I thought of noting down some of Sidi Brahim's maxims that he had passed on to me. But at the effort, the pen begins trembling in my fingers, the letters of my handwriting expand, coil, crawl over the walls. The inscriptions come alive, menacing, and then, suddenly calmed, they sing in an ancient and soothing voice:

'Cursed be the world and its unfolding, for life is created for pain. . . . Behold! – life is an enemy to men, yet they adore it!'

No, this is no cloistered meditation, no cold thought, but an enchanting song which penetrates me and arouses in me a profound emotion, as if some spirit were speaking to my spirit, instructing me, 'Forget!'

And it's as if my soul is a great fount, spilling over from a surfeit of these words: 'The world flows towards the grave as night flows toward the dawn!'

But I know still other songs, distant friend, lullabies so sweet and charming that, if you were singing them to your little beloved, she would snort with laughter at you, for your little beloved has never had fever. She knows only how to admire herself in a pocket mirror, fluttering her eyelashes and pursing her lips.

What's more, I'm sure she has luxuriant hair and the loveliest smile in the world, an intelligent smile. Her understanding is all an act. When her eyes roll back in ecstasy and her eyelids are creased and ringed with blue, don't go believing that at least she loves you: it's just a little tremor of egoism surfacing.

And why should she love you, you whose love, like mine, is nothing but a passionate endurance, while hers is a light-hearted joy? Therefore sing to her, to make her smile, lullabies composed for other idols that resemble her.

This evening these litanies of love have taken over my heart – a symphony of words, overlaid on the *zawiya*'s silence. . . . Despite all my efforts at attention, I never saw the singer's lips move.

It was a traveller. He said to me, 'Listen to this Egyptian song.' And then it was his eyes that spoke to me, yes, nothing but his mortal eyes:

'Before the threat of the Indian sword my gaze is always steady. – Before the gleam of my beloved's dark eyes, my gaze is troubled and forced to earth.

'Like the eye of the eagle, my eyes have never been dazzled by the sun. – The face of my beloved has muddled my reason and my sight.

'For as long as she was near, though unreachable, I was

[110]

happy. – We mortals cannot reach the stars, yet we love to contemplate their brilliance.

'And now that she is gone, my reason flies, my tears well up from my heart to my eyes, and flow from my eyes on to the sand. . . .'

I would like to fall asleep to these voices, listening both to the one keeping watch at my bedside as well as to those who sang on horseback, near me, one morning as we crossed the glaring *hamada*:

'Give me news of my beloved. Is she alive or dead? If she remembers and pines for me, I will die, – and then let her tears wash my corpse.

'And if she has forgotten me, if she's laughing and playing, undoing her hair, I will die, – and then let her hair be my shroud.'

African Influences

The fever has left me by stages, but I am still tired and not up to much activity. It's been a long time since I've received any letters, and I don't expect any more. I work at writing my impressions of the south, my meanderings and inventories, without knowing if these pages, written for their own sake, will ever interest anyone.

I wanted to possess this country, and this country has instead possessed me. Sometimes I wonder if this land won't take over all her conquerors, with their new dreams of power and freedom, just as she has distorted all the old dreams.

Is it not the earth that makes men?

What will become of the European empire in Africa after a few centuries, when the sun will have slowly assimilated and adapted the newcomers to the profound rhythms of African

[111]

climate and soil? At what moment will our northern races be able to call themselves indigenous, like the brown Kabyles and the Berbers with their pale eyes?

These questions often bother me. I'll think about them later. Or others will answer them for me.

One thing I'm convinced of is that it's useless to struggle against deep and irreducible causes, and that a lasting transposition of civilization is not possible.

African emanations – I breathe them in the warm nights like an incense forever climbing toward mysterious and cruel divinities. These idols will never be completely repudiated. They will keep appearing, monstrous, in nights of fever to all who come to lie on this earth, intending to sleep there, their eyes in the cold stars.

Moghreb

What solace there is, what heavenly relief when the sun goes down, and the shadows of date palms and walls lengthen, creeping forward along the earth to eclipse the glare.

My dejected indifference, born of daylight and illness, lifts; once again my eye is charmed and eager for the recurring splendour of a familiar scene. The simple beauty of this country with its sober lines becomes adorned with warm, transparent colours. The sterile soil becomes refulgent, transforming the foreground's monotony, while diaphanous mists drown the distances.

All living things, wilted and worn down a moment ago, revive now, suddenly taller and lovelier. This gentle, consoling renaissance of the soul takes place every evening.

In the gardens, the last hour of daylight heat slips away deliciously for me in tranquil contemplations, or in lazy conversations broken by long silences.

At *moghreb*, when the sun has set, we go to pray in the *hamada* beyond the cemeteries and the shimmering whiteness of Lella Aicha's *koubba*. All is calm, everything dreams and smiles in this enchanted hour.

Women pass by, going barefoot towards Ain Sidi Embarek. Men who were chatting, sprawled on the ground, stand up with the extraordinary nobility that comes over them at this daily resurrection.

A chorus of murmured prayer goes up from this corner of the desert dominated by the *ksar* and the Barga.

The prayer finishes, groups linger on their spread burnous, black and red prayer-beads slipping through fingers, lips chanting softly the Prophet's litanies.

To be healthy in body, cleansed of all dirt after lavish baths in fresh water; to be simple and to believe, never having doubted, never having fought oneself, in fearless, patient expectation of eternity: in this lies peace, a Muslim's happiness — and, who knows? — perhaps even wisdom.

Here the unchanging hours glide by with the sweetness and tranquillity of a river through a plain, where nothing is reflected except swarms of colours which pass today and will return tomorrow, to astonish us time after time.

Little by little, I've been feeling all my regrets and desires evaporating. I have allowed my mind to be emptied and my will to be stilled. Dangerous, delicious torpor, leading insensibly but surely to the brink of annihilation.

These days and weeks in which nothing happens, nothing is accomplished, in which no effort is even attempted; no trials to undergo, hardly any thoughts to think — must I erase this time from my existence, deploring its emptiness? Or, after the inevitable disillusionment, will I lament them as the best hours, perhaps, of all my life?

I don't know anymore.

To the extent that I feel myself saturated by ancient, unshaken Islam, which here seems to be the very breathing of the earth; to the extent that my days go by calmly, the necessity for labour and strife is less and less real to me. I who so lately dreamed of voyaging ever farther, who always wanted to be doing, have come to desire, shyly, cautiously, that this momentary intoxication and quiescence might last, if not always, at least for a long time yet.

But I know too well that the travelling fever will overcome me, and I will go. Yes, I know I'm still very far from the serenity of fakirs and Muslim hermits.

What urges me, though, to restlessness and keeps thrusting me on to life's roads, is not the wisest voice in my soul; it is a side of me that finds the earth too limited, and is unable to find in myself a sufficient universe.

What so many dreamers have searched for, simple people have found. Beyond science and the progress of centuries, I can see as under a lifted corner of a curtain into ages to come, and the future man who dwells there. And I understand too that one could end one's days in the peace and silence of some southern *zawiya*, end in ecstasy, free of yearnings, confronting only radiant horizons.

Reflections on Love

I should have liked to pass the summer at Kenadsa, leaving only to follow my road towards yet more distant and unknown countries. The Tafilala nomad tempted me. A caravan of Berbers, for five hundred French francs, felt they could guide me there without running any risk.

I would have set forth fearlessly with these people, confident of them and their word, but the debilitating fever comes and goes, so that I still lack the necessary energy and stamina.

To return to Ain Sefra and seek hospital care would be the most rational thing – and yet I can't bring myself to do it. I linger in my retreat; I breathe with delight the air that has poisoned me; I close my eyes to past and future, as if I had just drunk the magic water of oblivion and wisdom.

It's just that I've truly shaken off all yearnings. In moments of calm and reflection it occurs to me that here I have reached the very end of my wandering, tormented existence. A vast serenity has taken root in me, as if after a difficult ascension I have finally left behind the storm zone and encountered clear skies.

It's not easy to explain the state of mind which I have attained here. I'm not interested in analysing myself, still less in showing off. I have no audience! It seems to me that everything I say is very simple. The distance that I can now ascertain between my present way of seeing and the social aspirations such as newspapers and modern novels take for granted, comes no doubt from a geographic illusion, from my having broken through into the past, across countries frozen in time.

Here are a few conclusions I came to in solitude, one day when I was trying to see clearly into my heart, right through all the memories:

All love of an individual, carnal or fraternal, is slavery, a more or less complete effacement of the personality. One renounces oneself to become a couple.

The great delight felt in possessing another is also a great sacrifice.

Love and passion, however, are distinguishable. Sensual passion is not all coarseness. The Moroccan *taleb*, pale with *kif*, was no dissolute who intoned, 'I have searched for myself and exhausted my body in order to lighten my soul.'

The most deceiving and pernicious love of all seems to me the western tendency towards the 'sister soul'.

The beautiful, devouring, Oriental flame has nothing in common with equality and fraternity between the sexes.

The Muslim can love a slave and the slave can love her master. This authentication of the natural order completely reverses social systems.

Although it's rare that, at some detour on our way, a being similar to oneself should appear – someone recognizable and somehow familiar – when it happens our meagre self is unexpectedly exalted. We start believing in the possibility of completing ourselves, doubling ourselves, we extend our arms towards our own image . . . towards this, our true love . . . our true weakness!

Let us love above ourselves, let us love still more one who is beneath us. Let us elevate to ourselves the one who's willing to adore us, or let us be willing to desire our own elevation.

When I have felt my heart beating in true sympathy, outside of myself, it was in nature or in humanity – never in the throes of passion. So I have guarded myself during sexual abandon. Poor, I have possessed divine wealth, investing my most intoxicating pleasure in the magic of a flaming sunset over terraces of a desert village.

It is just that, at such moments, I am the heart of the earth; a surge of immortality flows through my veins; my chest expands with its force; I am free, existing above death. If then someone were to lean over me, to murmur 'my sister', all I could do would be to weep.

Glory to those who go alone into life! However unhappy they may be, they are the strong and the holy, the only beings. . . . The others are nothing but half a soul.

This state of mind should not be mistaken for asceticism. I

believe, rather, that I have found a great talisman of purity, permitting whoever possesses it to pass through any condition of life unsullied by any contact:

'Never give your soul to a creature, because it belongs to God alone; see in all creatures a motive for rejoicing, in homage to the Creator; never seek yourself in another, but discover yourself in yourself.'

And of course the most ignorant of beings will already be very knowledgeable if, like every good Muslim, he can unite without sin Faith with Sensuality.

I remind myself that we already spoke of these things in Algiers, before the immensity of the sea glittering in the moonlight, on certain nights one spring. They seemed quite natural to us in a setting of wanton sensuality, accompanied by 1001 cigarettes, in the presence of that young woman, brown and detached, her neck resting on the divan cushions, who knew how to listen, all ears and eyes, an exemplar of Oriental beauty who could smile at us and display herself to advantage.

One of us even declared that Faith was nothing but an obstacle. . . . But sensuality, even as interpreted by the highest form of art, could never contain all the soul's transports.

Today all that is far, very far from me, and I would love to know what others of our now dispersed little group think of it.

In my southern solitude, bygone words have grown up; they have taken on more of an interior value. I have connected them, in their new-found meanings, to so many plays which lead me back irrevocably to the ancient ages of the world, to epochs when the voice of sage and prophet still resounded; whereas the noise of today's literary tinklings passes unnoticed in the uproar of the street.

And I bless again my solitude which lets me believe, which fashions me into a being both simple and exceptional, resigned to her destiny.

Departure

I awaken for the last time on this terrace, to the *mueddin*'s hoarse call wailing in the night.

It's cool. Everything sleeps.

El Hassani and Mouley Sahel get up. Like me, they must leave this morning, but in the opposite direction.

I am bound for Bechar, Beni Ounif, and back to Ain Sefra to nurse myself in some fashion for the rest of the summer, so as to take advantage of the first autumn convoys.

Then I hope to proceed all the way to the Touatian oases. These regions are not unknown, but there has been almost nothing of value written, no useful observations about life there. This, I hope, will be my wintering place.

I'll return from there with notes which will complete another book of my impressions of the districts south of Oran and my musings about the *zawiya*. Like so many others, I too will have been an explorer, and those who come after to these countries will recognize the truth of what I've written. Some of my comrades, officers and soldiers of the south, will be able to augment them with the thousand trivialities of our discussions. The *mokhazni* with whom I've lived, simpler men, indifferent to written words, will hardly recognize my name. But when I return to them, they will think I only left them the day before. We'll resume our café chatter, and on our desert rides they'll be able to sing me their laments. Lassitude and disenchantment will come after a few years. . . . There's my future, straight ahead, or at least the one I like to envisage on this beautiful morning, just brightening, about to break on the day of my departure from Kenadsa.

Meanwhile my companions are also getting ready for their trip to Bou Dnib. They would like to take me along, and I wish I had the strength to follow them.

'Think about it, Si Mahmoud,' El Hassani tells me, 'there is still time. We'll travel for a whole month, crossing countries with numerous opportunities for you to see things and gain instruction. We will go up the Guir all the way to Tafilala or even to Tisnit. Everywhere you'll be received as our brother.'

The temptation is great. . . . But to leave as I am, this weak, and without official authorization, without notifying anyone . . . my journey – for study and to satisfy my curiosity – would surely be misconstrued. Torn over the matter, I resign myself to set off for Bechar today.

'No, El Hassani, I can't. This will be for later, in a while. When I'm able, I'll let you know.'

'May God assist all your undertakings!'

How different my return trip will be from the previous one, when I was travelling towards the unknown!

Two other blacks, who will be going on foot, are seated motionless against the wall, their rifles on their knees. They barely understand Arabic, for they were born and raised on the Fez road, among the Ait Ischorouschen, the roughest and least accessible of the Berber tribes.

One of them keeps a sullen silence and glances my way furtively. In his eyes, evidently, I am just a reprobate, a damned *M'zani*.

On a brief order from El Hassani, the negroes saddle the horses. He and Mouley Sahel point out the direction of the Guir, where they are heading. But they won't leave me just yet. They plan to accompany me a little and afterward retrace their steps.

'We will go with you as far as the entrance to the cemeteries,' says El Hassani.

We start off. My throat is so tight with emotion that I can hardly answer when I'm spoken to. And it's so important that I maintain to the end a manly courage.

Sharp, small paving stones are planted in the field, like slates in the hard clay, marking the graves with ledges. The horses, accustomed to them, can walk between these stones without striking them with their hooves. Here we dismount, as is the custom when friends must separate, and embrace each other three times.

'Go in God's peace and protection.'

'May you meet with no evil.'

Astride our horses once again, we depart in opposite directions: El Hassani towards the unexplored west, where I would like so much to follow him, and I towards the disenchantment of the familiar.

From the top of a knoll, I watch for a long time the diminishing figures of the Berbers from Bou Dnib. They disappear finally in the labyrinth of dunes, under the pink radiance of daybreak. With them fades away my last ray of hope: it will be a long time, if ever, before I can penetrate further into Morocco.

While my mare advances slowly, I gaze broken-heartedly over the valley which had struck me as so beautiful when I entered it from the opposite direction, in the heady newness of summer. And because I'm going backwards, into what may be a long exile from my much loved desert, I find the landscape mediocre, almost ugly, bristling with a thousand peaks which fail to capture any light, or my eyes. Its charm has vanished.

My legs flail against Souf, forcing her into a mad gallop, and I let my tears be dried by the desert wind. . . .